OCS Study
MMS 2003-049

Deepwater Observations in the Northern Gulf of Mexico from In-Situ Current Meters and PIES

Volume II: Technical Report

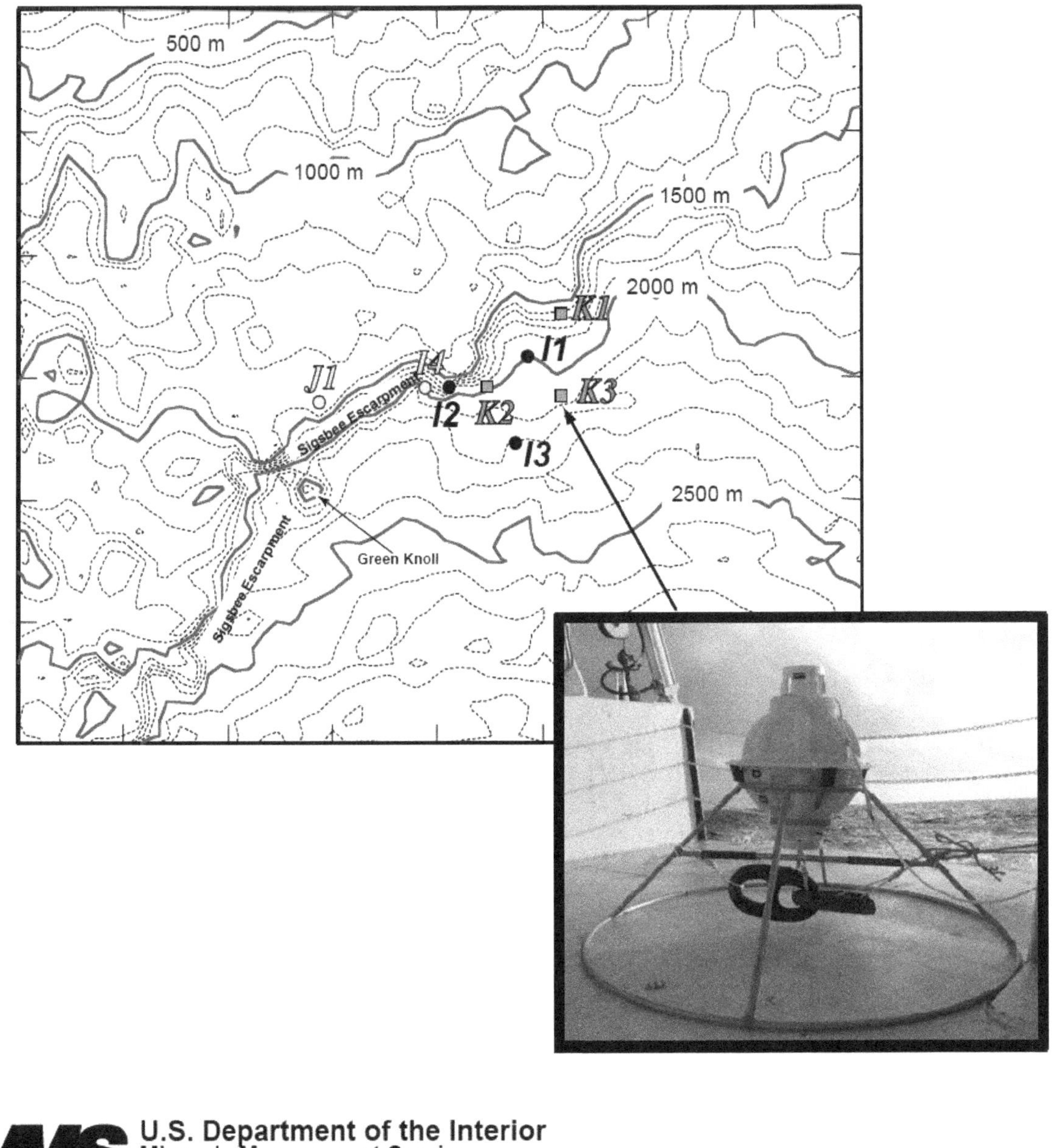

MMS U.S. Department of the Interior
Minerals Management Service
Gulf of Mexico OCS Region

OCS Study
MMS 2003-049

Deepwater Observations in the Northern Gulf of Mexico from In-Situ Current Meters and PIES

Volume II: Technical Report

Authors

Peter Hamilton
James J. Singer
Evans Waddell
Science Applications International Corporation

Kathleen Donohue
University of Rhode Island

Prepared under MMS Contracts
1435-01-00-CT-31132
and
1435-01-96-CT-30825
by
Science Applications International Corporation
615 Oberlin Rd., Suite 100
Raleigh, North Carolina 27605

Published by

U.S. Department of the Interior
Minerals Management Service
Gulf of Mexico OCS Region

New Orleans
August 2003

DISCLAIMER

This report was prepared under contract between the Minerals Management Service (MMS) and Science Applications International Corporation. This report has been technically reviewed by the MMS, and it has been approved for publication. Approval does not signify that the contents necessarily reflect the views and policies of the MMS, nor does mention of trade names or commercial products constitute endorsement or recommendation for use. It is, however, exempt from review and compliance with the MMS editorial standards.

REPORT AVAILABILITY

Extra copies of the report may be obtained from the Public Information Office (Mail Stop 5034) at the following address:

U.S. Department of the Interior
Minerals Management Service
Gulf of Mexico OCS Region
Public Information Office (MS 5034)
1201 Elmwood Park Boulevard
New Orleans, Louisiana 70123-2394

Telephone Number: 1-800-200-GULF or
504-736-2519

CITATION

Suggested citation:

Hamilton, P., J.J. Singer, E. Waddell, and K. Donohue. 2003. Deepwater Observations in the Northern Gulf of Mexico from In-Situ Current Meters and PIES. Final Report. Volume II: Technical Report. U.S. Dept. of the Interior, Minerals Management Service, Gulf of Mexico OCS Region, New Orleans, LA. OCS Study MMS 2003-049. 95 pp.

ABOUT THE COVER

The map shows the Sigsbee Escarpment south of New Orleans that was the primary focus of measurements from instruments on the indicated moorings. Moorings I1-4 and J1 were normal tautline moorings. Moorings K1-K3 were Inverted Echo Sounders with Pressure (PIES). The picture is of a PIES on the back deck of the mooring deployment vessel. The "orb" contains all the instrumentation associated with operations and recovery of the instrument. The stand is used in regions where strong bottom currents are expected, such as the present study area.

ACKNOWLEDGMENT

The insight of Dr. Willis Pequegnat was verified with this project. One of the authors remembers well listening to Willis many years ago describe how his biological sampling gear lowered near the present study area could not reach the bottom due to very strong bottom currents.

Both the MMS and BP provided support to this measurement program. This cooperative funding was essential to acquisition of the resulting horizontal and vertical coverage as well as the measurement duration. Dr. Alexis Lugo-Fernandez, the MMS COTR, and Mr. David Driver, the BP representative, worked cooperatively to define a program that accomplished both industry and government objectives.

TABLE OF CONTENTS

LIST OF FIGURES

LIST OF FIGURES (continued)

LIST OF FIGURES (continued)

LIST OF FIGURES (continued)

LIST OF FIGURES (continued)

LIST OF TABLES

xv

1.0 INTRODUCTION

As an extension of the MMS-Funded DeSoto Canyon Eddy Intrusion Study (Hamilton et al., 2000) additional current/temperature measurements were made at the base of a Sigsbee Escarpment in water depths of approximately 2000 m. Deepwater and near-current measurements in this specific area, supported by BP, indicated the occurrence of periodic higher speed events that could be of considerable importance to expected oil/gas exploration and development in this deepwater area. In order to have available representative and pertinent knowledge of conditions in these development areas, the MMS funded a series of fairly site-specific, deepwater current measurements. In conjunction with MMS support, BP provided support to expand the depth and areal coverage of these measurements in what was a cooperatively government-industry measurement program.

The specifics of the various components of measurement program and a characterization interpretation of many of the key attributes of the observations are presented in this report.

1.1 Background

In August 1999, the Minerals Management Service (MMS) funded the deployment of an array of three moorings, clustered near the 2000 m isobath at the base of the continental slope, south of the Mississippi delta (Figure 1-1). This array was designed to study energetic deep currents that had been previously observed by a mooring deployed for BP Exploration Inc. in Block 618 of the Atwater Valley lease area (Hamilton, 1998). Both the previous BP mooring and the MMS array were situated south of a relatively steep slope known as the Sigsbee Escarpment which is an extensive approximately east-west geological feature across the deep northern slope between the Mississippi delta and east Texas. The MMS array consisted of one, extensively instrumented, full depth mooring (I1) and two short bottom moorings (I2 and I3). In order to discover how far up the slope high speed deep currents might extend from the Atwater site, BP funded another short bottom mooring on a block (Green Canyon 782) north of the escarpment (Figure 1-2). This mooring, denoted J1, was deployed in conjunction with the three MMS moorings. This four mooring array was deployed in August 1999. Mooring J1 was retrieved in August 2000 after one rotation in January 2000. Moorings I1, I2, and I3 were redeployed and after a further rotation in February 2001, finally retrieved in September 2001. During the final six months, BP and MMS jointly funded the near bottom moorings at I1, I2, I3 measurements and another deep mooring, named I4, on the middle part of the escarpment, just west of I2. The MMS also supported extending Mooring I1 from a near bottom to a full depth mooring. During these final six months, the MMS further supported deploying three Inverted Echo Sounders, equipped with precision bottom pressure sensors (known as PIES), positions approximately equidistant from the full depth mooring, I1. These positions are denoted K1, K2 and K3. These latter were deployed to use PIES to estimate measurements of temperature and salinity depth profiles, and through the geostrophic equations combined with bottom currents on absolute velocity profiles. The gravest empirical mode (GEM) method is used to convert travel time between the bottom mounted PIES and the surface, and back, to salinity, temperature and density profiles (Watts et al., 2001). Pairs of density profiles can then be used to compute geostrophic velocity profiles (He et al., 1998).

1

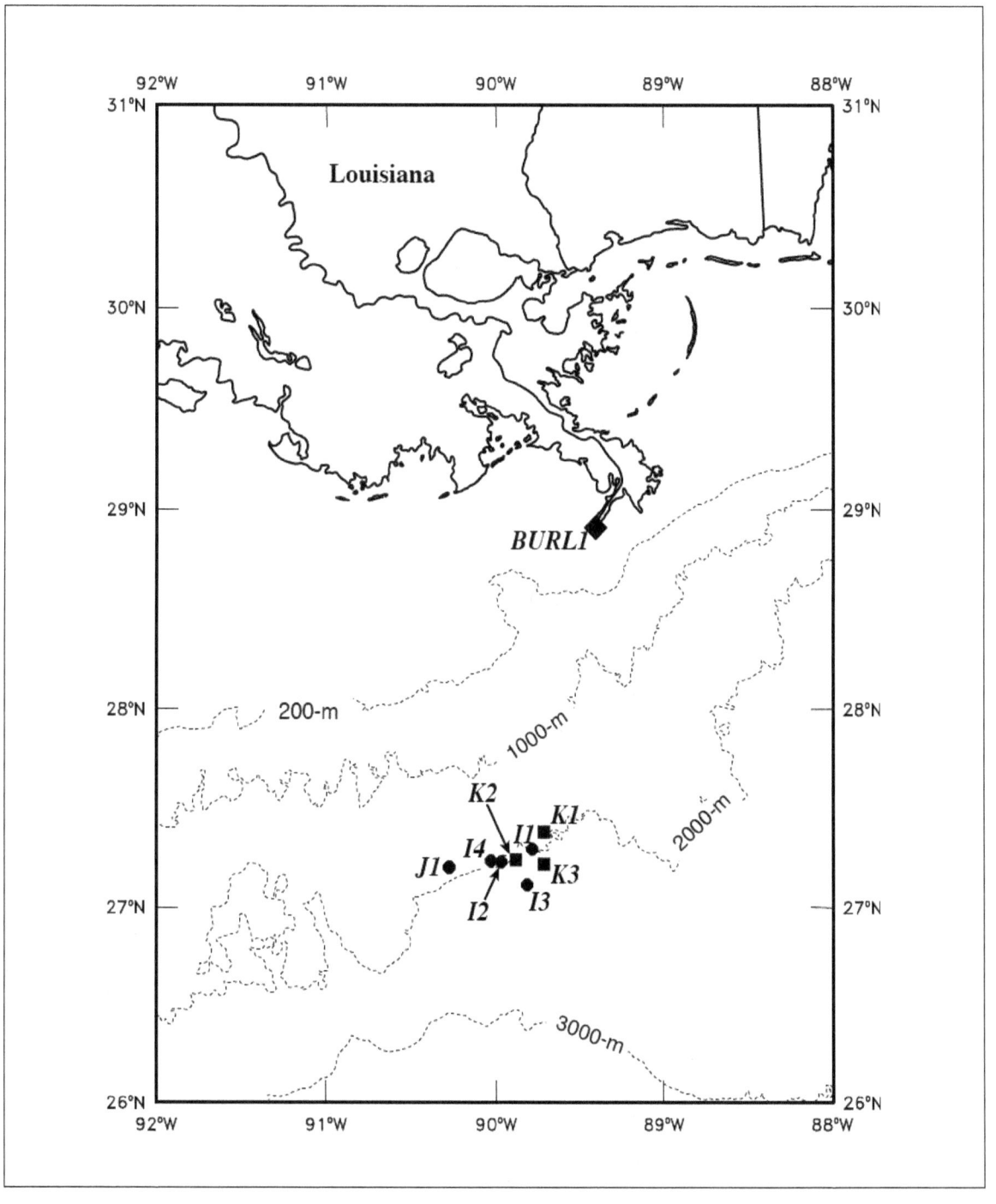

Figure 1-1.   Map of the deployment region in the northern Gulf of Mexico. Solid dots and squares are the positions of current meter moorings and bottom-mounted PIES, respectively. The C-MAN meteorological station at Southwest Pass, LA is indicated by the solid diamond.

2

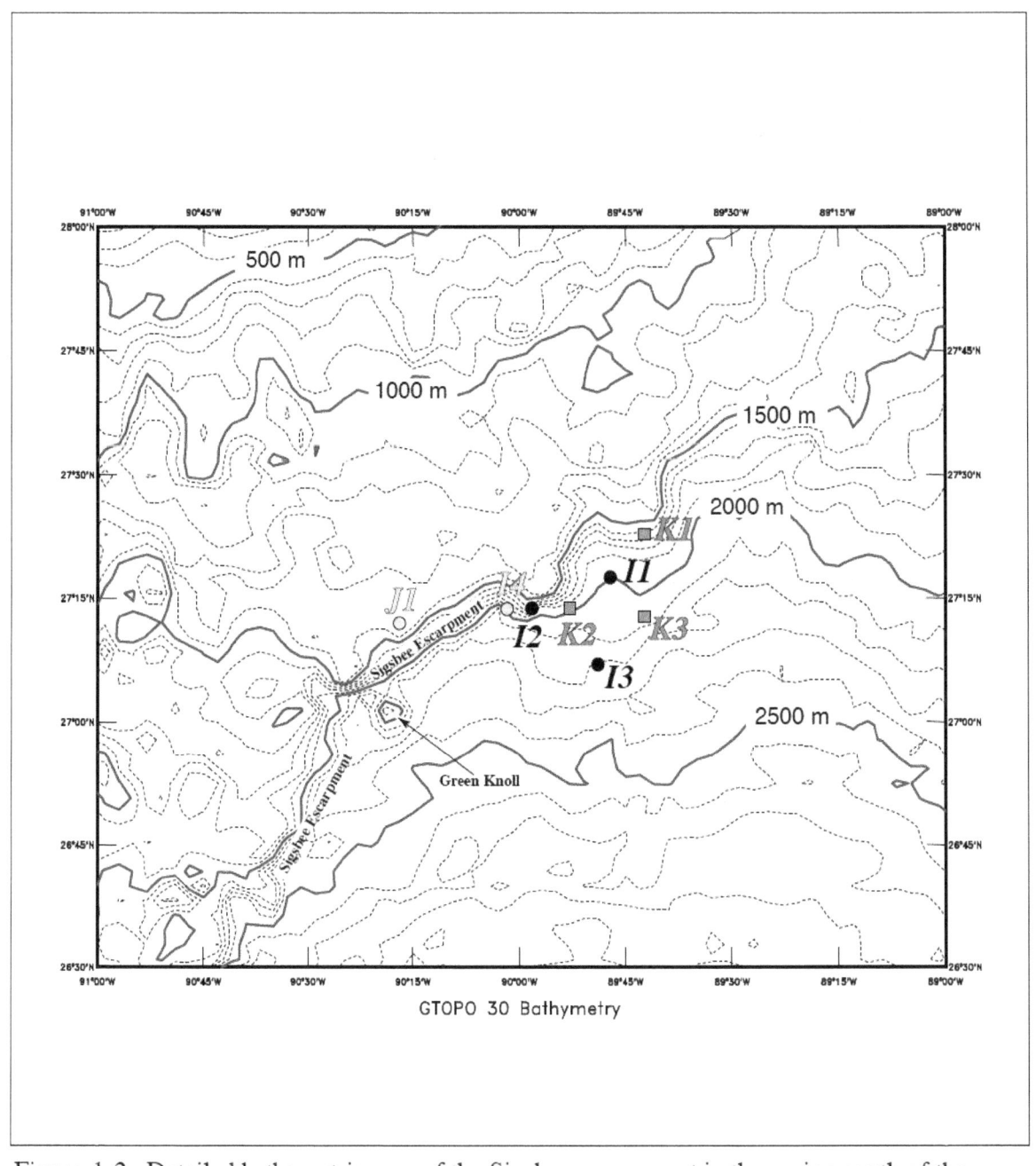

Figure 1-2. Detailed bathymetric map of the Sigsbee escarpment in the region south of the Mississippi delta. The positions of the MMS moorings (I1, I2 and I3, black circles) and PIES (K1, K2 and K3, red squares), and the BP moorings (J1 and I4, green circles) are shown.

3

Such derived profiles can be compared to the time series measured at I1. Successful use of PIES would allow economical mapping of low-frequency current, salinity and temperature profiles over larger regions of the deep Gulf of Mexico than might be possible using conventional current meter moorings. PIES have been used successfully, for this purpose, in many regions of the world's oceans (e.g., Sun and Watts, 2001; Howden et al., 1994; Kelly and Watts, 1994). This report discusses the measurements made at all moorings and PIES over the two-year period. A discussion of the first six months of current measurements is given in Hamilton and Lugo-Fernandez (2001). Aspects of the first year of bottom currents at I1, I2, I3 and J1 were also analyzed in a report to BP by Hamilton et al. (2000).

Observations of the water column over the deeper portions in the Gulf of Mexico basin indicate that there is a basic two-layer structure. Above ~800 to 1200 m depth, the circulation is dominated by the Loop Current (LC) in the east, anticyclonic rings shed from the Loop Current in the central and western basin, and smaller-scale cyclones and anticyclones that are probably generated by the LC rings. This upper layer has vigorous flows that result from eddies, and interactions between eddies. These flows often have strong vertical shears (Kirwan et al., 1984; Elliott, 1982; Hamilton, 1992).

Below ~1000 m, eastern Gulf measurements have shown that currents are nearly depth-independent with a tendency for bottom intensification. These lower-layer flows do not appear to have a strong relationship to simultaneous current fluctuations in the upper layer. Hamilton (1990) suggested that these deep motions may result from topographic Rossby waves (TRW) propagating westward across the continental slope and rise of the basin. Similar kinds of deep motions have been extensively studied in the Mid-Atlantic Bight where there is evidence that they are generated by meanders of the Gulf Stream (Hogg, 1981; Pickart, 1995). In the Gulf, it seems plausible that deep TRW's are generated by Loop Current fluctuations, Loop Current eddy (LCE) shedding events, and the propagation of LCE's across the Gulf. The latter could include the interaction of LCE's with topography and other eddies in the basin. However, the generation mechanisms of TRW's are not presently well understood.

Previous analyses of deep current data, from the BP Atwater 618 block (Hamilton, 1998) and the MMS moorings (Hamilton et al., 2000; Hamilton and Lugo-Fernandez, 2001) were also interpreted in terms of TRW's. However, these current magnitudes were exceptional (~ 50 cm/s) and the periods were short (~ 10 days) compared to other regions of the central and western Gulf. A source for such short period TRWs was not obvious. Current measurements made on a single mooring under the LC showed almost no energy at periods shorter than about 15 days (Hamilton, 1990). It was speculated that LC/LCE frontal eddies had space and time scales that matched the observed high-frequency TRW's and therefore could be a source (see Pickart, 1995). In a recent paper, Hogg (2000) has also observed energetic, short period TRW's on the western flanks of the Grand Banks in the North Atlantic. He attributed these TRW's to transient behavior of the Gulf Stream as it passes over the tail of the Grand Banks, though direct evidence of this mechanism was lacking. The analogy with the LC extending over the Mississippi fan is striking, and thus, similar phenomena may be responsible for both the Gulf and North Atlantic TRW motions.

1.2   Organization of the Report

Chapter 2 discusses the database of measurements used in this report. It includes a basic description of the characteristics of the observed current, temperature and salinity fields. Analysis and statistics of the observations are given in Chapter 3. The results from the PIES and the comparison to the moored data at I1 are discussed in Chapter 4, and the study is summarized in Chapter 5.

2.0 CURRENT MEASUREMENTS

2.1 Data

Instrumentation on each of the moorings is shown in Table 2-1 with locations shown in Figure 1-2. Each instrument has an ID of the form *DSC-xx-#,* where xx is the mooring ID (e.g. I1) and # is the number of the instrument from the top of the mooring. Because of the number of instruments on I1, where # > 9, letters of the alphabet are used (e.g. A through O). Because the instrumentation changed slightly between deployments, the additional or replacement of instruments on I1 have instrument numbers or letters that are out of sequence. Time lines of the data return for all instruments are given in Figure 2-1. Note that six of the instruments are ADCP's that measure velocity profiles at intervals of either 4 or 8 m. These instruments were directed to measure profiles up or down from their positions on mooring I1 (see Table 2-1.). All instruments in the lower layer (depths > 800 m) were conventional current meters.

All data records underwent basic quality assurance during which suspect data values were flagged. Current records were corrected for magnetic variation. Short gaps of a few hours caused by flagged data or the rotation of the moorings were subsequently filled by linear interpolation. Long gaps of up to 2 days were filled with a proven procedure that preserves the spectral content and has similar energy levels to the rest of the records. In the mooring rotation gaps (mainly for I1), care was taken that the vertical coherence between levels were similar to other portions of the mooring's records. This is particularly important for the closely spaced depth levels generated by the ADCP's. The records at each depth level were merged into continuous time series where possible. The original data was recorded at 30 or 60-minute intervals and show varying degrees of noise in the records. To minimize this, all records were filtered with a three-hour low-pass (3-HLP) Lazcos kernel and decimated to 1-hour intervals. The axes of the current velocity records were rotated so that the V-component was directed along the general trend of the isobaths. A rotated record has the notation Rθ after the ID, where θ is the clockwise rotation angle of the V- or along isobath component from true north. The U- or cross-isobath component is then directed at angle θ+90°. To analyze efficiently the current motions with periods greater than one day that dominate deepwater flows, the 3-HLP records were further filtered with a 40-HLP kernel and resampled at 6-hour intervals. The processing and calibration of the PIES is given in Chapter 4.

2.2 Methods

Methods for analyzing time series generally follow established techniques such as those used by Hamilton (1990) to characterize TRW motions in the deep Gulf. These include spectra, coherence and phase calculations, and EOF or principal component analysis (PCA). Spectra are used to determine the periods (frequency bands) of the energetic motions. Coherence squared and phase differences show the relationships between pairs of spectra. EOFs provide information on the coherent spatial structures associated with a frequency band using multiple records. Spectra are calculated by standard FFT methods that allow record lengths that are not a power of 2. The time series are demeaned and a 10% cosine taper applied before the FFT. The

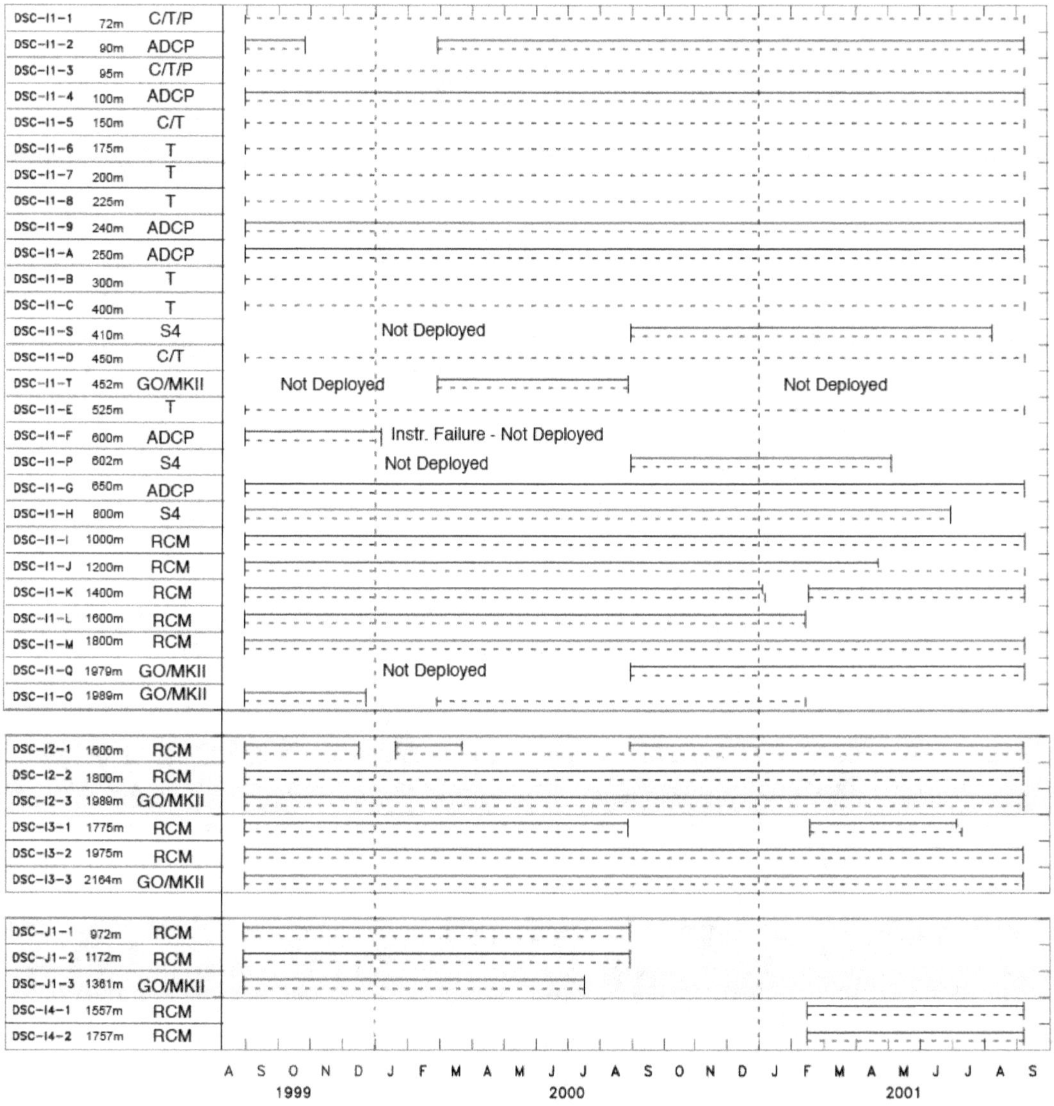

Figure 2-1. Time lines of data return for the current meter moorings. Solid and dashed lines represent velocity and scaler (e.g. Temperature and Salinity), respectively. On Mooring I1, a 150 kHz, up-directed ADCP failed near the end of the first six months and was replaced by various in-situ current meters for the remainder of the mooring deployments.

Table 2-1. Moored instrument and PIES measurement levels for the DeSoto Canyon Extension Program.

Mooring	Water Depth (M)	Instrument Depth (M)	Instrument Type
I1	2000	72	C/T/D
		90	ADCP (300 kHz) - up
		95	C/T/D
		100	ADCP (300 kHz) - down
		150	C/T
		175	TEMP (Mini)
		200	TEMP (Mini)
		225	TEMP (Mini)
		240	ADCP (300 kHz) - up
		250	ADCP (300 kHz) - down
		300	TEMP (Mini)
		400	TEMP (Mini)
		410	S4 (Deployments 3 and 4 only)
		450	C/T
		452	MK2 (Deployment 2 only)
		525	TEMP (Mini)
		600	ADCP (150 kHz) (Deployment 1 only) - up
		602	S4 (Deployments 3 and 4 only)
		650	ADCP (75 kHz) - down
		800	S4 (+ 75 kHz ADCP Overlap)
		1000	RCM-7 (+ 75 kHz ADCP Overlap)
		1200	RCM-7
		1400	RCM-7
		1600	RCM-7
		1800	RCM-8
		1979	MK2 (Deployments 3 and 4 only)
		1989	MK2
I2	2000	1600	RCM-7/MK2
		1800	RCM-7
		1989	MK2
I3	2175	1775	RCM-7
		1975	RCM-7/MK2
		2164	MK2
I4	1950	1550	RCM-7
		1750	RCM-7
		1939	MK2
J1	1372	972	RCM-7
		1172	RCM-7/MK2
		1361	MK2
K1 (1NE)	1771	1770	PIES
K2 (1W)	2060	2059	PIES
K3 (1SE)	2108	2107	PIES

raw spectral estimates are smoothed using a rectangular Daniel window (Koopmans, 1974). EOF in the frequency domain uses spectra from multiple time series to separate the spatial and frequency content in terms of orthogonal modes. Preisendorfer (1988) has given a comprehensive treatise on EOFs.

2.3   Upper-Layer Event Description

The I1 mooring site was strongly impacted by major Loop Current anticyclones and sometimes the LC itself. Peripheral eddies that translate along the fronts of these major features also frequently affect the study location. To place the measurements in context, a brief description is given of the major features found in the upper-layer records that can be related to circulation events observed by remote sensing. Figure 2-2 shows selected 40-HLP velocity records in the upper 800 m of the water column. Included in Figure 2–2 are the salinity and temperature 40-HLP records from the main thermocline at 150-m depth. At the beginning of September 1999, the LC was well extended to the northwest with the main front just east of the site (Figure 2-3a). A regular sequence of warm and cold events accompanied by rotating current vectors occurred. The cold and warm events were accompanied by generally westward and northward flows, respectively. This is consistent with a sequence of frontal eddies with warm crests and cold troughs propagating northwards along the LC front. Figure 2-3a suggests the existence of these cold (negative SSH anomalies) features even though they are poorly resolved by the altimetric maps. The warm and cold events had large and small vertical shears, respectively. The more depth-independent velocities in the cold events were consistent with circulation in cold eddies (Berger et al. 1996; Hamilton et al. 2002). The extended LC shed a large anticyclone (named " Juggernaut") which moved slowly westward between October 1999 and February 2000. Eddy J was highly elliptical in shape and as it moved westward the major axis rotated clockwise. The consequence of this is that I1 was sometimes just outside the front and sometimes just inside with the eddy center about 100 to 150 km south of the mooring. The general rotation of the current vectors from northwards to eastward between October 1999 and February 2000 and the relatively high temperatures and salinities are consistent with this scenario (Figure 2-2a).

A particularly interesting event occurred around December 24, 1999. The current vectors rotated clockwise from east to south, and there was a strong cooling at depth that is shown in the isotherm contours (Figure 2-4). Figure 2-3b gives the SSH map for December 12, 1999. It shows a cold eddy, centered north of the site, on the northern side of Eddy J. This eddy subsequently moved rapidly to the southeast, in the direction of Eddy J's swirl currents, as Eddy J translated further to the west. The rapid rotation of the upper-layer current vectors is consistent with the southeastward translation of a cold eddy through the I1 mooring site.

During February 2000, Eddy J only peripherally affected the near-surface currents at the site and by the beginning of March it was centered about 26°N, 92°W (Figure 2-3c). Some large temperature fluctuations occurred in the surface layer at this time (Figures 2-2b and 2-4), but they only penetrated to about 400 m (Figure 2-4) and were accompanied by weak currents (Figure 2-2b). There is little sign of any peripheral eddy activity in Figure 2-3c, therefore it appears the upper 200 m was influenced by an anticyclone that was too small to be resolved by the altimetry.

10

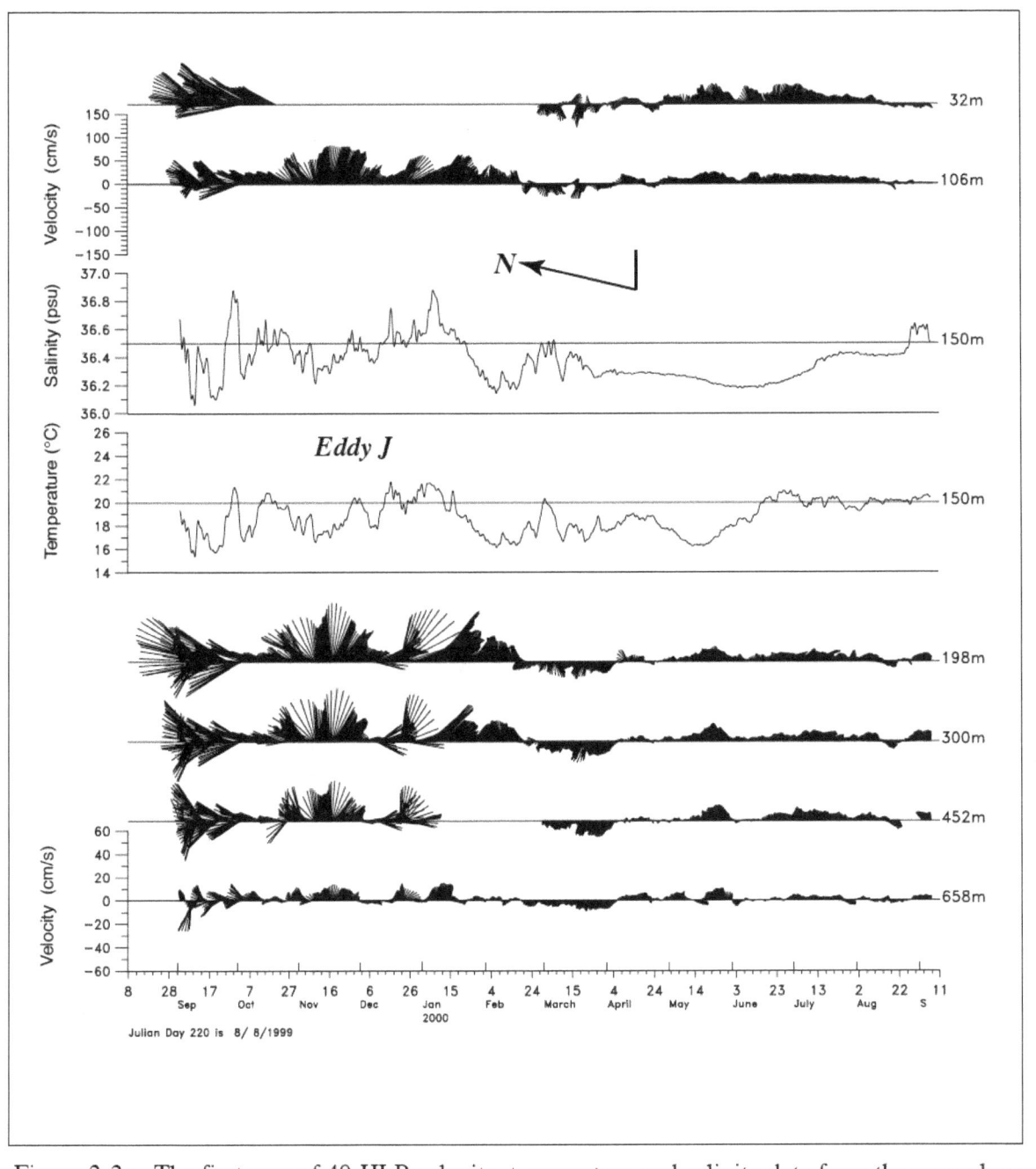

Figure 2-2a. The first year of 40-HLP velocity, temperature and salinity data from the upper-layer records at mooring I1 for the indicated depths.

11

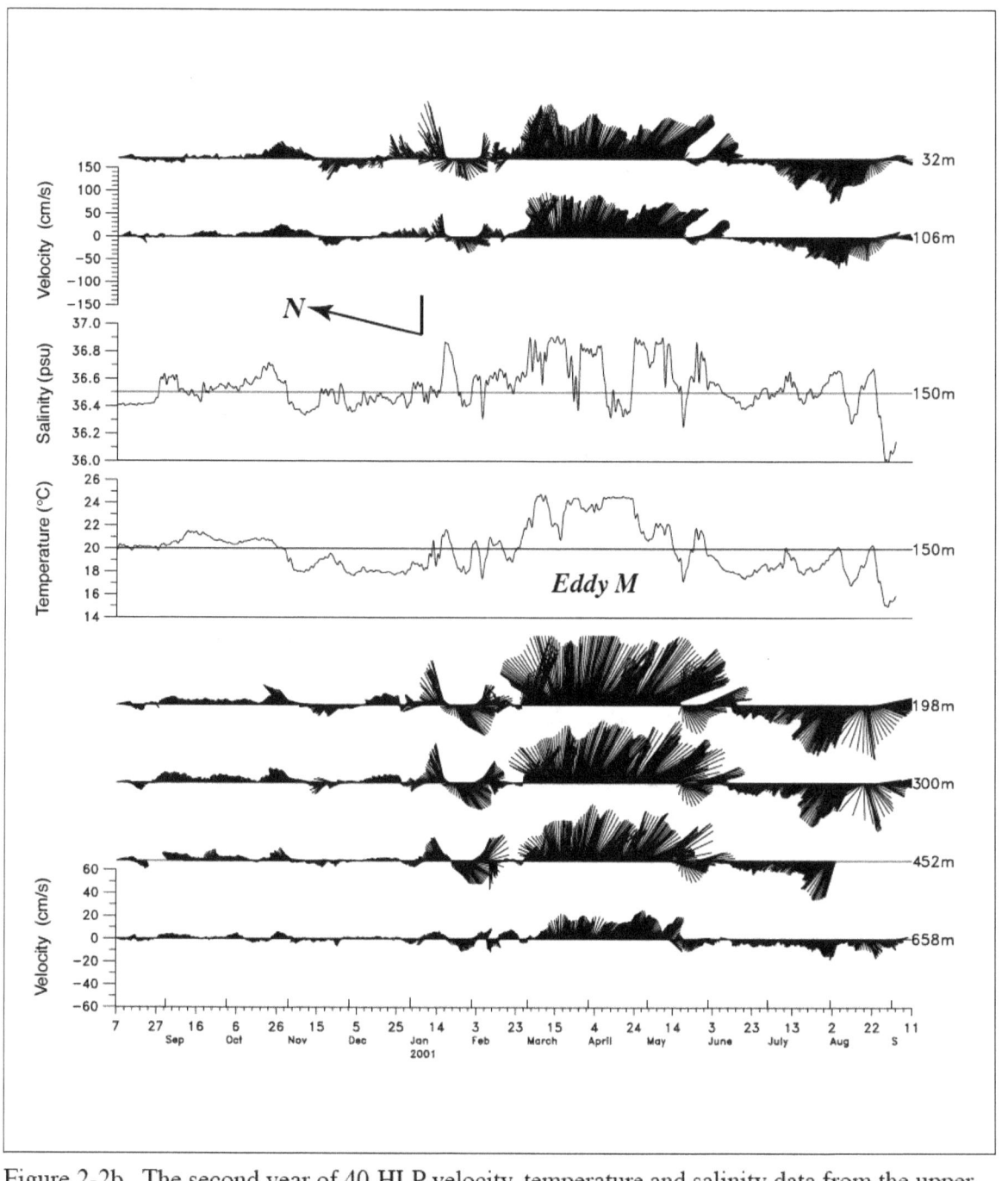

Figure 2-2b. The second year of 40-HLP velocity, temperature and salinity data from the upper-layer records at mooring I1 for the indicated depths.

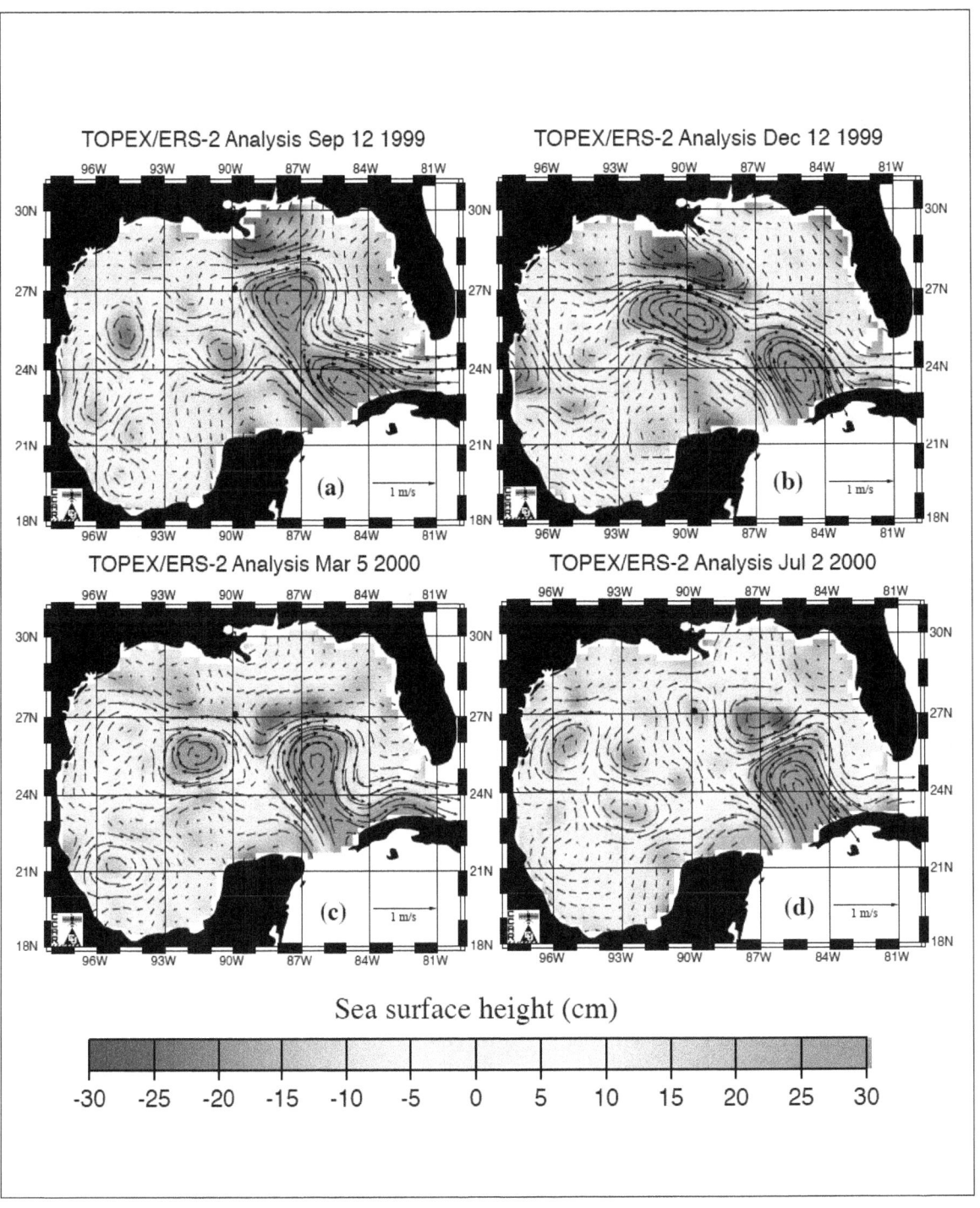

Figure 2-3a-d. Sea surface height anomaly maps from TOPEX/ERS-2 altimetric data (courtesy of R. Leben, CCAR). Geostrophic surface velocities are overlaid. The data is composited from about 7-days of satellite passes centered on the given date: September 12, 1999 (a), December 12, 1999 (b), March 5, 2000 (c), and July 2, 2000 (d).

Eddy J subsequently interacted and was partially absorbed by an old major anticyclone in the western Gulf (April and May, 2000). The LC did not retreat very far to the south when Eddy J was shed. It remained extended to the north for most of the first six months of the study (e.g. Figure 2-3b), and was probably still interacting with Eddy J up to the middle of December. During the middle of May 2000, a small LC eddy, that was highly elongated in the east-west direction, partially detached from the LC. This eddy was reabsorbed into the LC by the end of the month. However, as part of this process, a weak anticyclonic circulation was shed from the west-side of the LC. This anticyclone was named Eddy "Kinetic" (K) by the oil industry even though it did not qualify as a major LC eddy. By July, this weak anticyclone (Eddy K) had moved north and was centered over the mooring site (Figure 2-3d). Upper layer currents remained weak throughout this March through August, 2000 interval. When Eddy K began to affect the site in June 2000, the highest currents were observed in the upper 100 m along with a general warming of the water column (Figures 2-2b and 2-4). As Eddy K moved further over the site, the near-surface currents decreased and the deeper levels increased and then decreased as the center approached. Current magnitudes were generally less than 20 cm/s. This behavior is characteristic of a bowl shaped depression of the isotherms and associated geostrophic current field slowly moving across the study area. The maximum depth of the isotherms occurred at the beginning of July 2000 and it is noteworthy this was similar to the observed maximum depths that occurred during Eddy J. However, the center of Eddy J did not pass over the site and the depth of the 10°C isotherm would be expected to be 600 to 650 m in the center of such a vigorous eddy. It is also noteworthy that the salinity in the center of the weak eddy during July and August, 2000 only increased to ~36.4 psu. This implies that water from the core of the LC (salinities > 36.6 psu) was not incorporated into this anticyclone.

The marked contrast of the vigor of the current and temperature fluctuations between the first and second six months is clearly shown in Figures 2-2a and 2-4a. In the first interval, the upper-layer currents at the site were dominated by the peripheries of the LC and Eddy J. In the second half, Eddy J had moved away from the study area and the upper-layer flows were relatively quiescent. This distinction in the nature of the flows was not reflected in the deep current fields that are discussed in the next section.

The weak, warm Eddy K remained over the site until November 2000. It interacted with the LC and a large cyclone to the northwest of an extended LC. These interactions appear to have strengthened this eddy and the temperatures and salinities increased indicating that LC derived water had been entrained in this circulation. An example of these interactions is given in Figure 2-3e for September 24, 2000. In November 2000, Eddy K began to move westward and the cooling and weak southward flows indicate that the site was being influenced by the western side of a cold cyclone situated north of the LC (Figure 2-3f). At the beginning of January 2001, the LC front moved over the study site with northeastward currents, and high salinities and temperatures. This was followed by a peripheral cyclone (Figure 2-3g) that moved through the site towards the northwest. The current vectors (Figure 2-2b) rotated anticlockwise and the temperatures were relatively cool.

The high eastward and northeastward currents associated with a detaching LC eddy (known as "Millenium"), arrived over Mooring I1 in March 2001 and dominated the records for the next three months. After being shed, Eddy M was a moderate size, relatively circular LC anticyclone

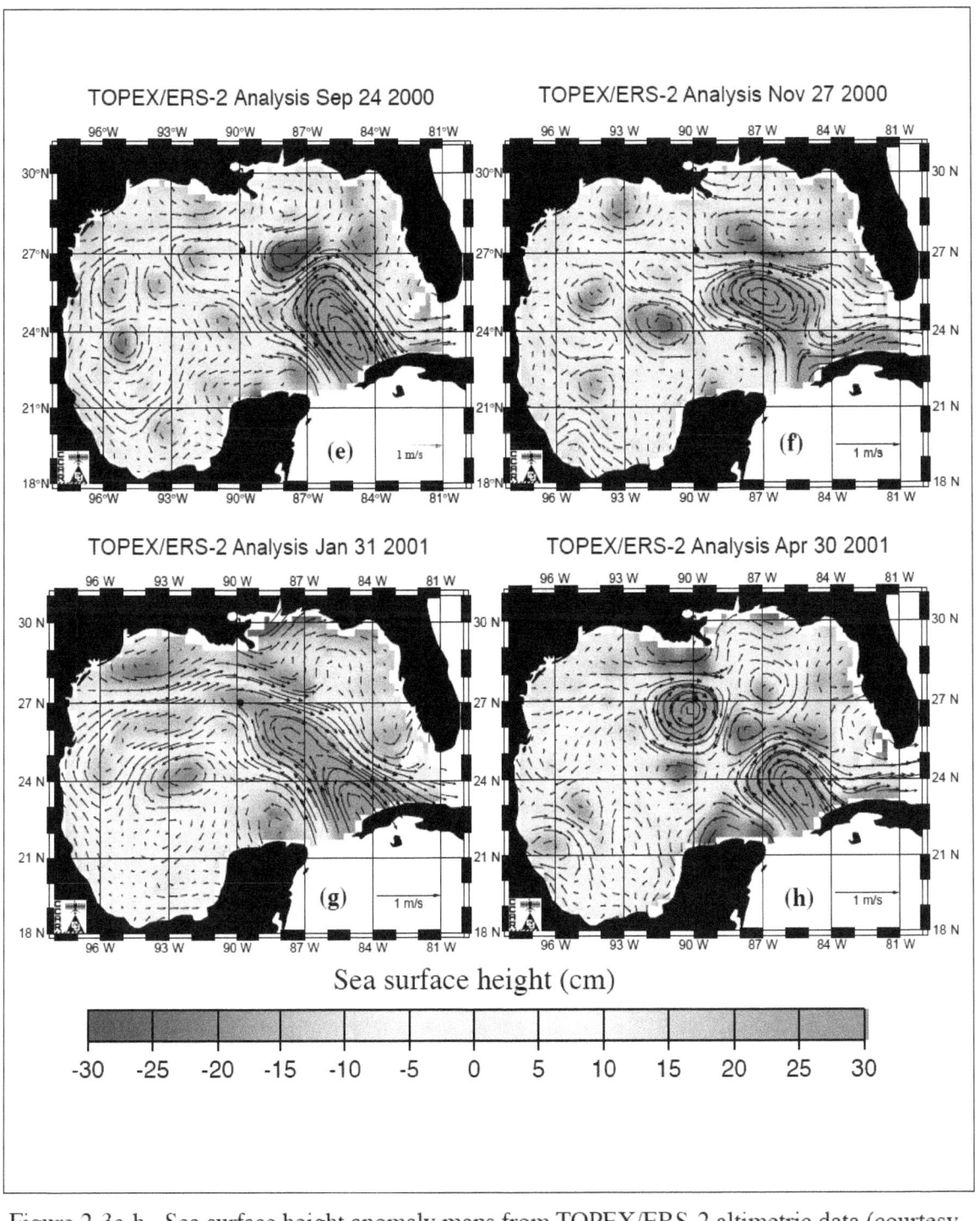

Figure 2-3e-h. Sea surface height anomaly maps from TOPEX/ERS-2 altimetric data (courtesy of R. Leben, CCAR). Geostrophic surface velocities are overlaid. The data is composited from about 7-days of satellite passes centered on the given date: September 24, 2000 (e), November 27, 2000 (f), January 31, 2001 (g), and April 30, 2001 (h).

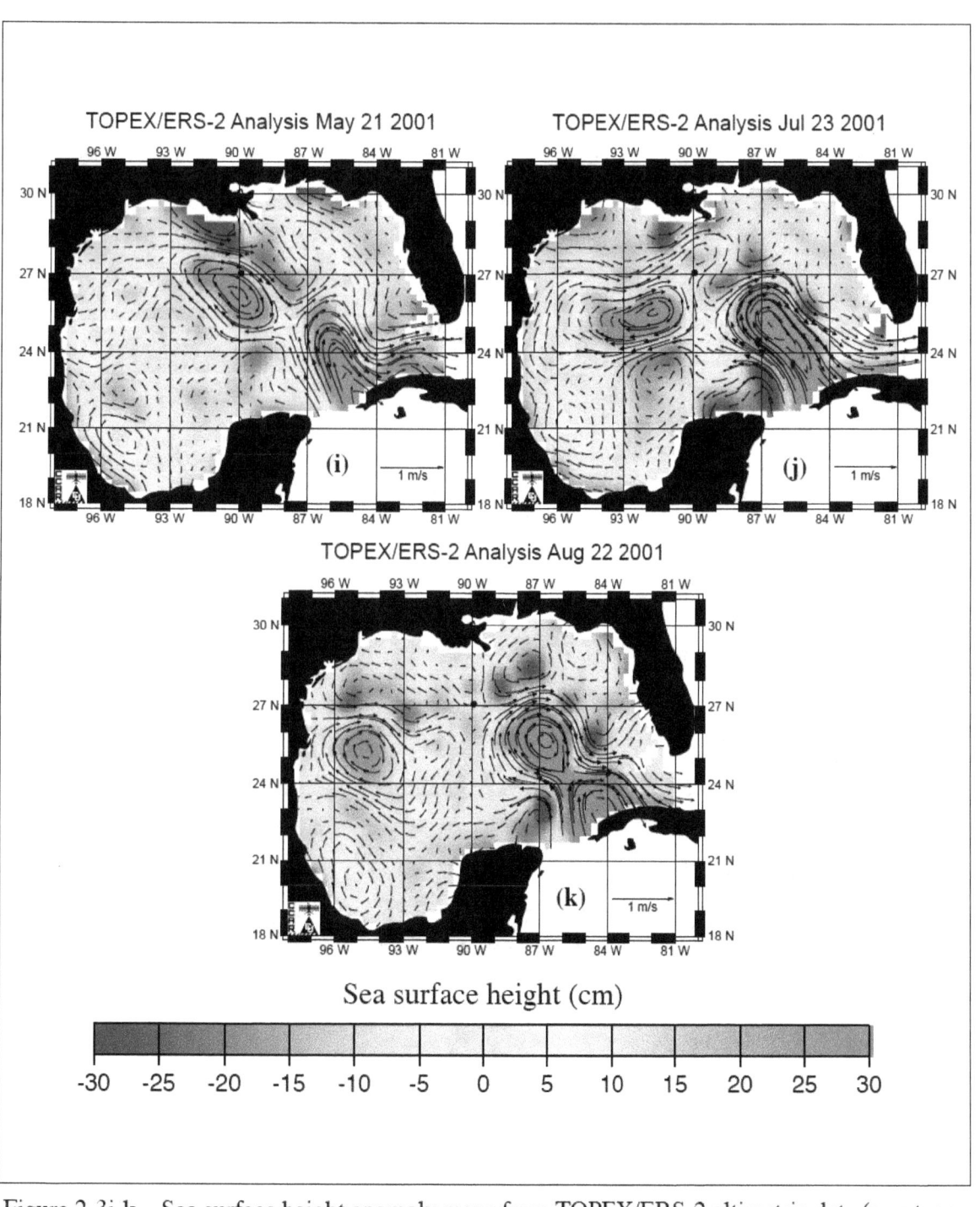

Figure 2-3i-k. Sea surface height anomaly maps from TOPEX/ERS-2 altimetric data (courtesy of R. Leben, CCAR). Geostrophic surface velocities are overlaid. The data is composited from about 7-days of satellite passes centered on the given date: May 21, 2001 (i), July 23, 2001 (j), and August 22, 2001 (k).

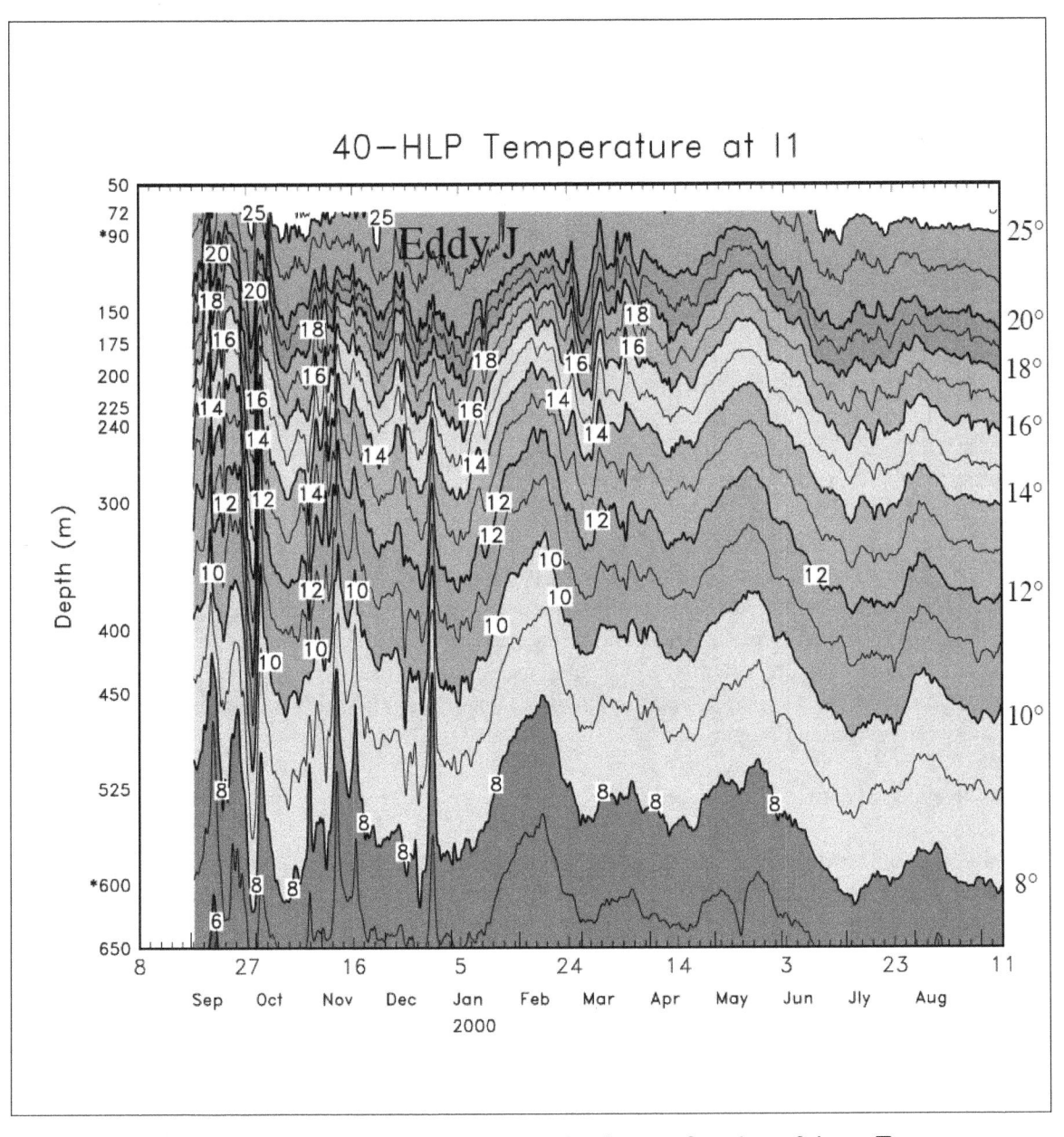

Figure 2-4a. The first year of upper layer isotherm depths as a function of time. Temperatures are in degrees Celcius. The depths of the 40-HLP temperature measurements used are indicated on the right side of the figure..

(Figure 2-3h). As with the passage of Eddy J, the upper layer temperature fluctuations (Figure 2-4b) were considerably more energetic than the previous 9 months (March 2000 to January 2001) when no major LC eddies were affecting the site. Similar to Eddy J, the center of Eddy K was south of the site and the displacements and the clockwise axis rotations of the eddy as it translated westward caused large changes in temperatures. However, the site was generally closer to the center of Eddy M than it was for Eddy J as can be seen by the greater depths (~ 600 m) of the 10°C isotherm in the former compared to the latter (~ 450 m). This is also shown by the generally higher salinities at 150 m during March through May, 2001 than in the earlier September 1999 through January 2000, interval. Eddy M moved away to the west-southwest and when the front was over the site there was a cold event through the upper water column around May 16, 2001 (Figure 2-4b). The current vectors rotated anticlockwise (Figure 2-2b) and the temperature and velocity signals were similar to the cold event in December 1999 when Eddy J was moving away from the site. The major axis of both eddies at the time of these events were directed northwest to southeast (Figures 2-3b and 2-3i). The implication is that this position and orientation of a major LC eddy was favorable for the rapid translation of frontal cyclones.

By early June 2001, Eddy M was no longer directly influencing the site. A cyclonic eddy on the northwest side of the LC caused the weak westward and southwestward flows in June and July 2001. These strengthened as this cyclone apparently interacted with a slope anticyclone (Figure 2-3j). In August and September, the vectors rotated anticlockwise and there were two cold events in the temperature records which may be interpreted as the cyclone moving off to the northeast, around the LC front, accompanied by an intrusion of the southern side of the slope anticyclone over the site (Figure 2-3k).

2.4   Deep Currents

The 40-HLP currents from the lower 1000 m of the water column at I1 are given in Figure 2-5. Currents and temperatures at 100 m below the water surface are also shown so that the lower layer currents can be compared to the presence or absence of major eddies. The lower layer currents were characterized by energetic fluctuations with periods of 10 to 20 days that persisted for several months. At I1, the amplitude of the fluctuations increased suddenly and then decayed slowly over several months. This can be considered to be characteristic of trains of wave-like energy propagating through the site. Motions were coherent through the lower 1000 m of the water column and there is evidence of larger magnitude currents closer to the bottom than at 1000 to 1200 m depth. This is known as bottom intensification and is characteristic of planetary motions known as topographic Rossby waves (Rhines, 1970). At least three of these energetic wave events can be identified in the two years of the records. The first event was already in progress when the moorings were deployed in September 1999. This generated some of the highest bottom speeds observed in the two-year study. A second possible event began in December 1999, coincident with the cold cyclone passage discussed above, but it is not clear if it can be considered as distinct from the earlier wave train. After a period of quiescence in February and March 2000, another energetic wave train appearred and the fluctuations persisted until at least the beginning of August 2000 (Figure 2-5a). Bottom current fluctuations were small from August through November. In December 2000, bottom speeds increased to about 20 cm/s and the fluctuations could be considered to be a weak wave train. However, in February 2001, a major event occurred, just prior to the arrival of Eddy M, which persisted through June

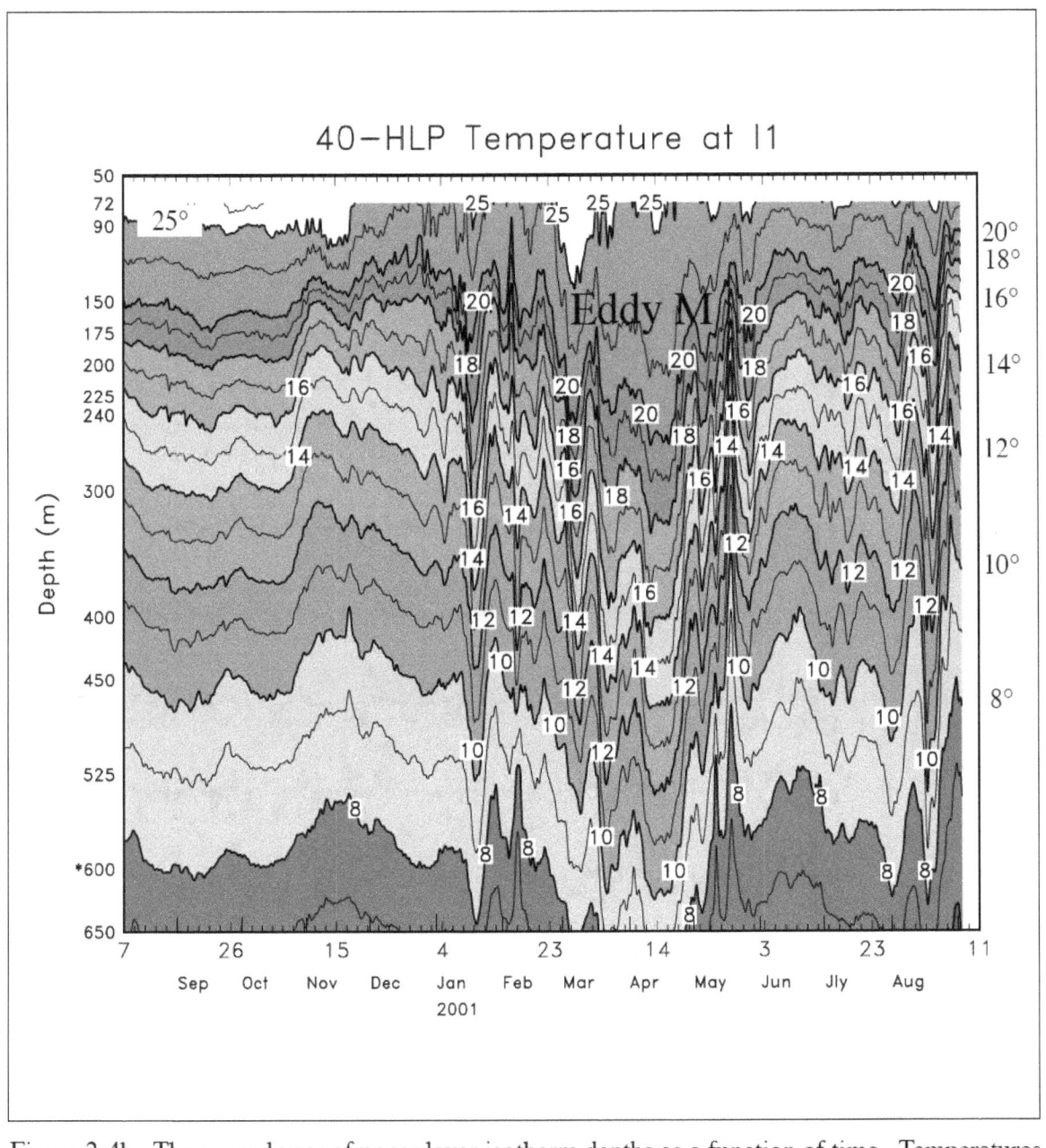

Figure 2-4b. The second year of upper layer isotherm depths as a function of time. Temperatures are in degrees Celcius. The depths of the 40-HLP temperature measurements used are indicated on the right side of the figure..

19

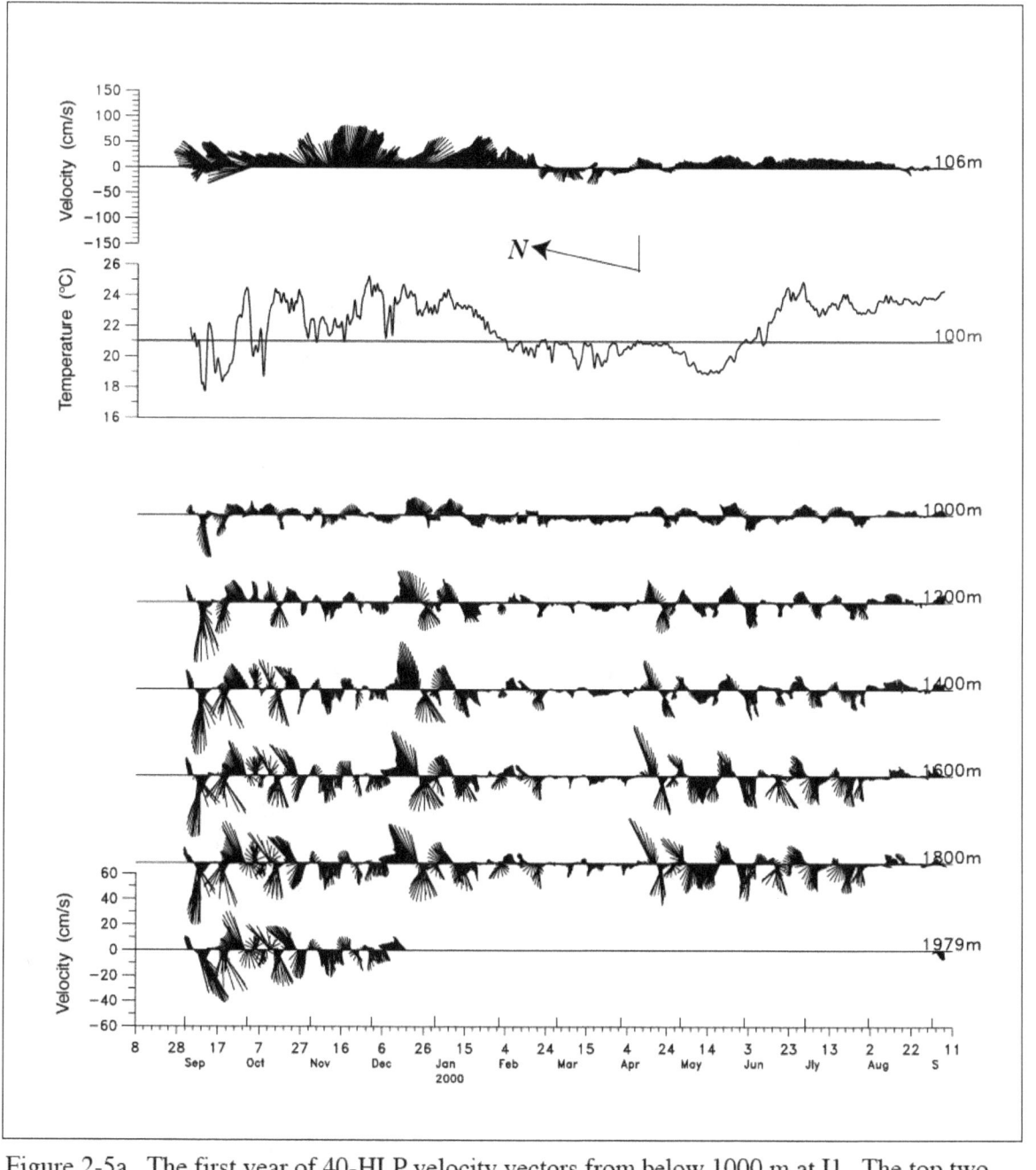

Figure 2-5a. The first year of 40-HLP velocity vectors from below 1000 m at I1. The top two panels show the velocities and temperature at 100 m depth.

(Figure 2-5b). Finally, at the end of the measurement period, in August 2001, the initial part of another energetic wave train was observed, again coincident with the passage of a cold cyclone. Thus, the lower layer currents at I1 were dominated by energetic events that persisted over several months separated by intervals of low amplitude fluctuations.

An important question is whether the waves in the lower-layer had have any relation to upper-layer flows. The September 1999 and February 2001 wave trains occurred when the upper-layers were dominated by Eddies J and M, respectively. The wave train occurred in April 2000 when there was no major eddy activity in the central Gulf (Figure 2-5). For most of the records the 1800 m and 100 m currents appear to have had little or no relationship. However, some of the major current fluctuations that occurred in September 1999, December 1999, February 2001 and August 2001, had a similar character to those of the surface-layer that were associated with cyclones moving through the site. In particular, the westward event around September 8, 1999 was similar at all depths at I1 (see also Figures 2-2a and 2-5a). Similar events were observed at all the bottom records at this time though there were some phase differences. There were also similar current fluctuations at all depths of I1 for the event around December 24, 1999. In this case the flows were eastward at all depths and were attributed to a cold cyclone interacting with Eddy J. In early February 2001, the initial, smaller amplitude fluctuations had some similarity with the anticlockwise rotating current vectors in the upper layer associated with a propagating peripheral cyclone (Figures 2-2b and 2-5b). However, the large eastward fluctuation around August 10, 2001 was in the opposite direction to the upper-layer currents at this time, even though they were again associated with a cyclone. These events suggest that occasionally there may have been connections between rapidly varying upper-layer flows and wave-like events in the lower-layer. However, these apparent relations could be just circumstantial with the observed waves propagating into to the region from distant sources. It is also difficult to test statistically the significance of such brief events where the currents appear to have had some coherence through the water column when in general the upper and lower level flows had very different characteristics.

The April 2000 wave train also showed some relation with the upper-layer currents (Figure 2-5a). However, the fluctuations at the 100 m level were smaller than at 1800 m on I1. This may be an indication of the lower-layer TRW activity penetrating up into the upper-layer when the latter is quiescent. There was no obvious large change in the configuration of the LC in this March-April period that could be considered as a possible distant source of such energetic waves.

Comparison of the lower-layer currents across the arrays (I1, I2, I3 and J1 in the first year, and I1, I2, I3 and I4 in the second year) shows how the wave energy changed with position and water depth. The 40-HLP lower-layer velocity vectors from the four moorings in each year are given in Figure 2-6. It is immediately apparent that the fluctuations on each mooring were highly coherent and thus the lower part of the water column moved like a slab. Mooring I2 had the highest amplitude currents, with I1 and I3 being a little less energetic and J1 and I4 considerably less energetic. The fluctuations at the deepest mooring, I3, were also a little more rotary than the strongly rectilinear fluctuations at the other moorings. The pattern of the fluctuations through time is also quite similar at all the moorings. The records begin in September 1999 with a burst of very strong currents. These events produced the highest speeds observed at I2 (Figure 2-7),

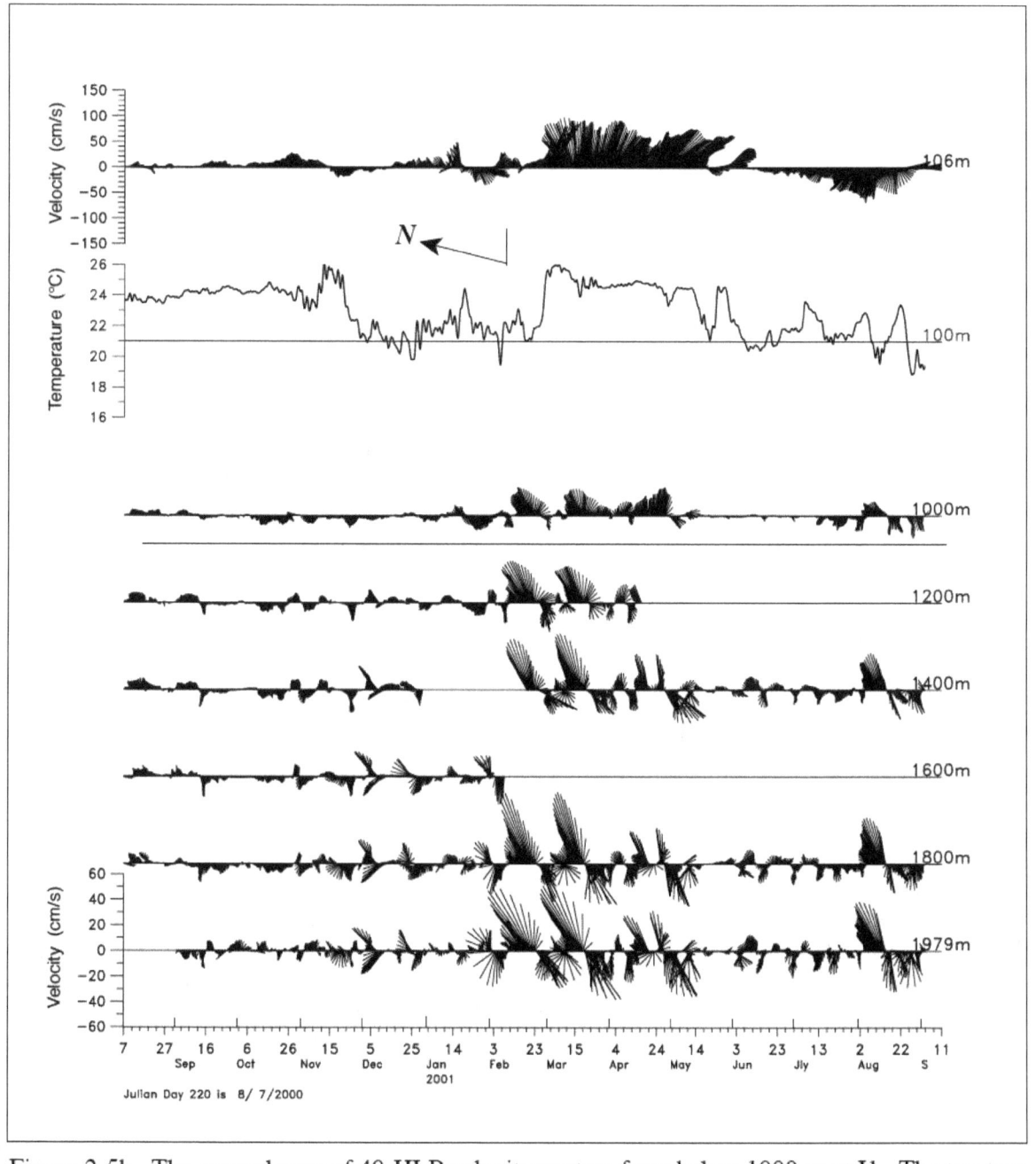

Figure 2-5b. The second year of 40-HLP velocity vectors from below 1000 m at I1. The top two panels show the velocities and temperature at 100 m depth.

22

and clearly the effect of the event was felt at J1 where the highest speeds of that one-year record was also observed. From these initial events, the energy slowly decayed through March 2000. The decay rates were not uniform across the array. The fluctuations persisted more strongly at I2 than at I3 and I1, and the decay at J1 occurred over a much shorter period. By the middle of October 1999, the maximum speeds at J1 were below 20 cm/s (Figure 2-7a).

In April 2000, the burst of energetic activity also had uneven distributions of magnitude and the change of activity with time also differ from the September 1999 waves. The April 2000 set of waves was again observed at all three I moorings though the maximum speeds were less than for the September 1999 events (Figure 2-6a). Again, I2 had the highest speeds and the high speeds persisted longer than at the other moorings. Some of the speed pulses were also observed at J1, but again their amplitudes were considerably diminished (Figure 2-7a).

In contrast, the February 2001 bottom currents at I1 had the highest speeds with more persistant high speeds at I3 than occurred in the previous wave trains. Again, the energetic fluctuations continued at I2 much longer than at the other two moorings and seem to merge with the August 2001 event (Figures 2-6b and 2-7b). Current amplitudes at I4 were considerably reduced over those at I2 during the last six months of the records. I2 and I4 were separated by a distance of only 6 km, with I4 having been slightly higher (50 m) up the escarpment slope (Figure 1-2). It is clear that the higher speed events at I4 (> 25 cm/s) occurred only for eastward flows at both I2 and I4. The speeds at I2 were approximately double those at I4. This very large change in short distance implies very strong horizontal shears and strong influence by the local topography of the escarpment slope. It is possible that I4 was situated in a flow separation zone, however, flow directions at both I2 and I4 oscillated both eastwards and westwards, and because the change in magnitude was also observed at the upper current meters, which are 400 m above the bed, makes this unlikely (Figure 2-6b).

Interpretation of these bottom layer records in terms of TRWs is given in Chapter 3. This will include diagnosis of characteristic periods and how bottom-trapped the motions were. It can be seen that the amplitude of the record at 200 and 400 m from the bottom were often similar (Figure 2-6) implying a depth-independent flow. However, the dense instrumentation of I1 shows that the records at 800 and 1000-m from the bottom have weaker fluctuations than the deeper records. It is clear, however, that the major events of the first six-months are more barotropic than the fluctuations that began in April 2000 and February 2001 (Figure 2-5).

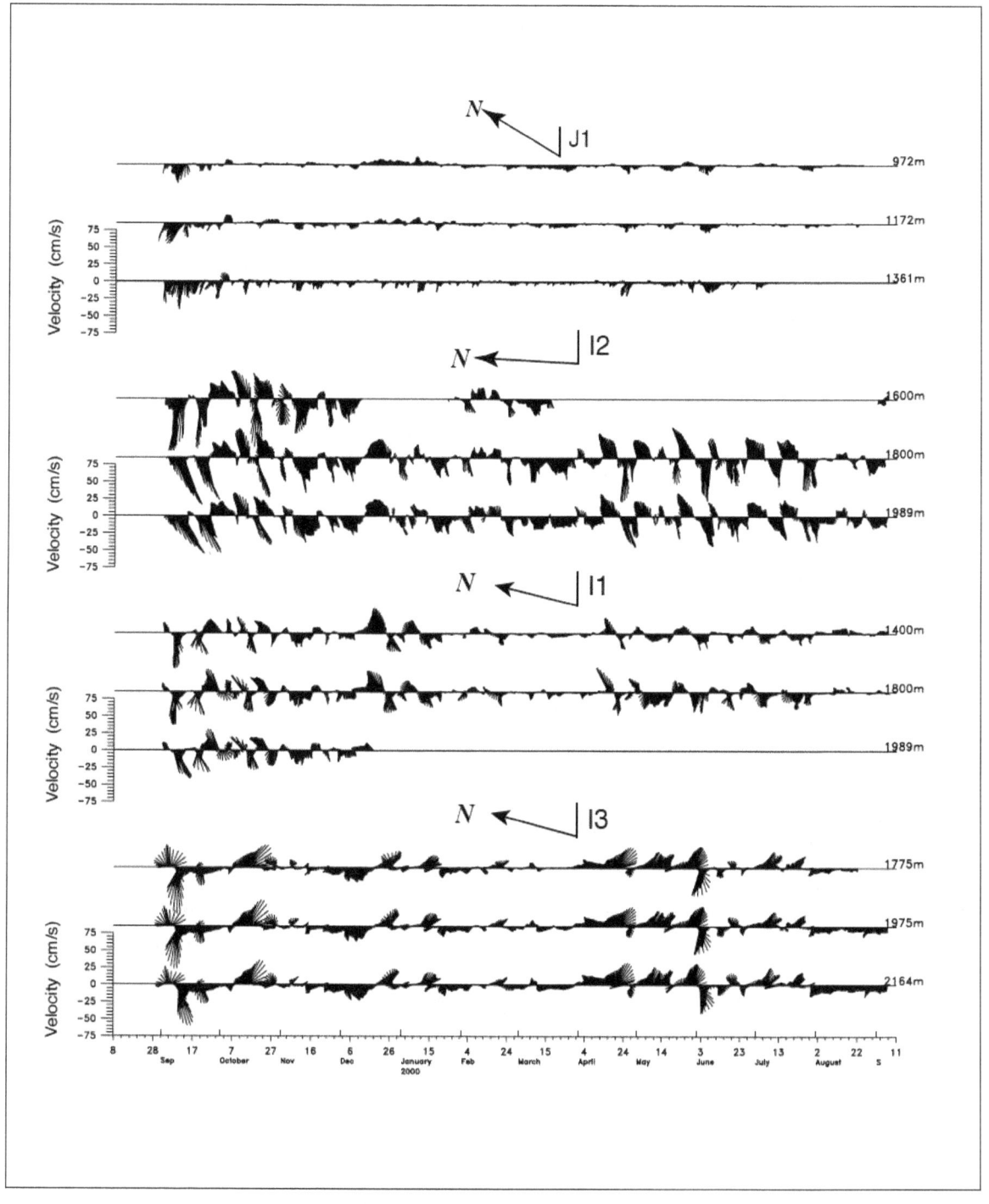

Figure 2-6a. The first year of 40-HLP velocity vectors from below 1000 m at I1, I2, I3 and J1. The direction of the y (V-component) axis with respect to North for each mooring is indicated.

24

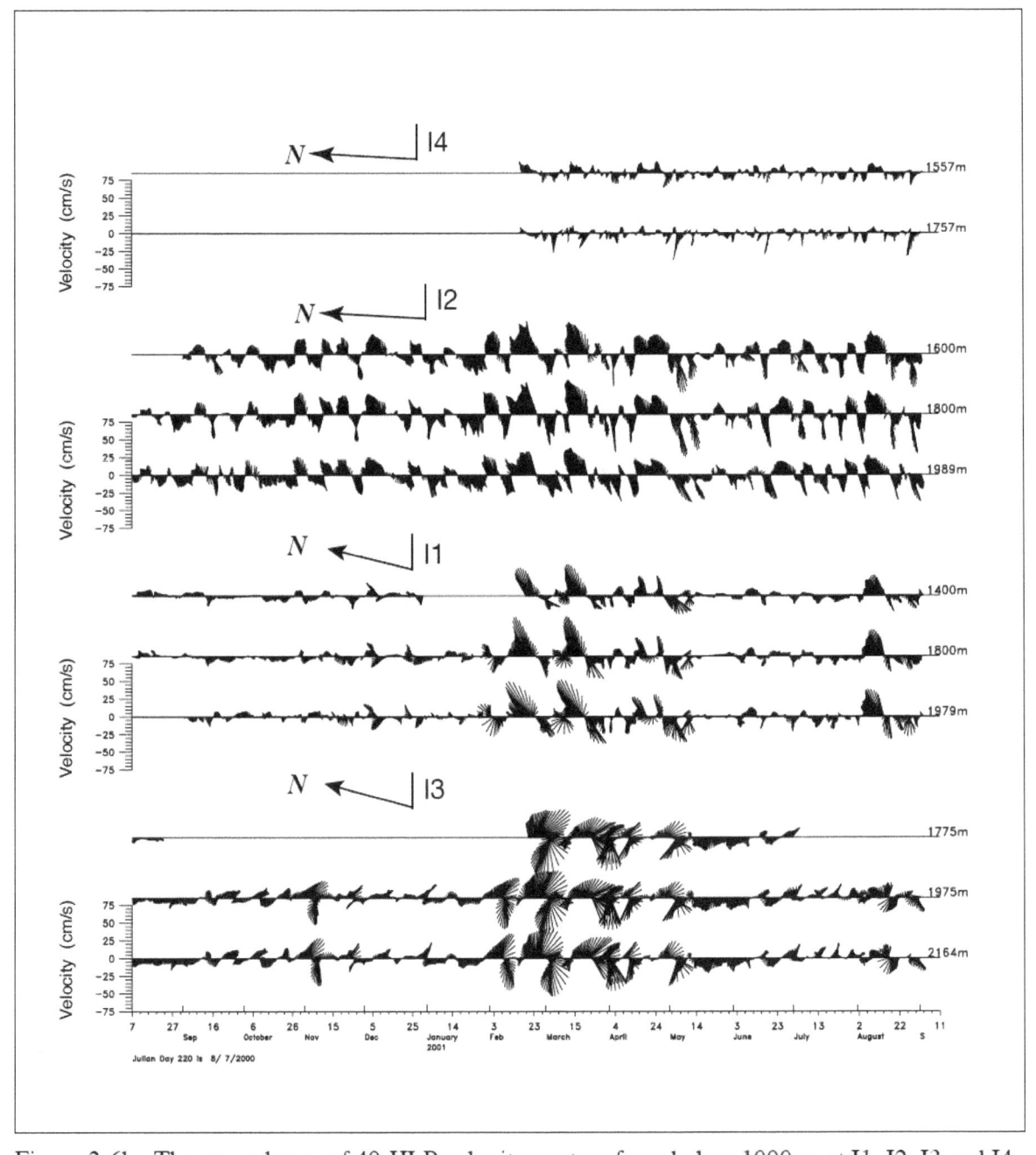

Figure 2-6b. The second year of 40-HLP velocity vectors from below 1000 m at I1, I2, I3 and I4. The direction of the y (V-component) axis with respect to North for each mooring is indicated.

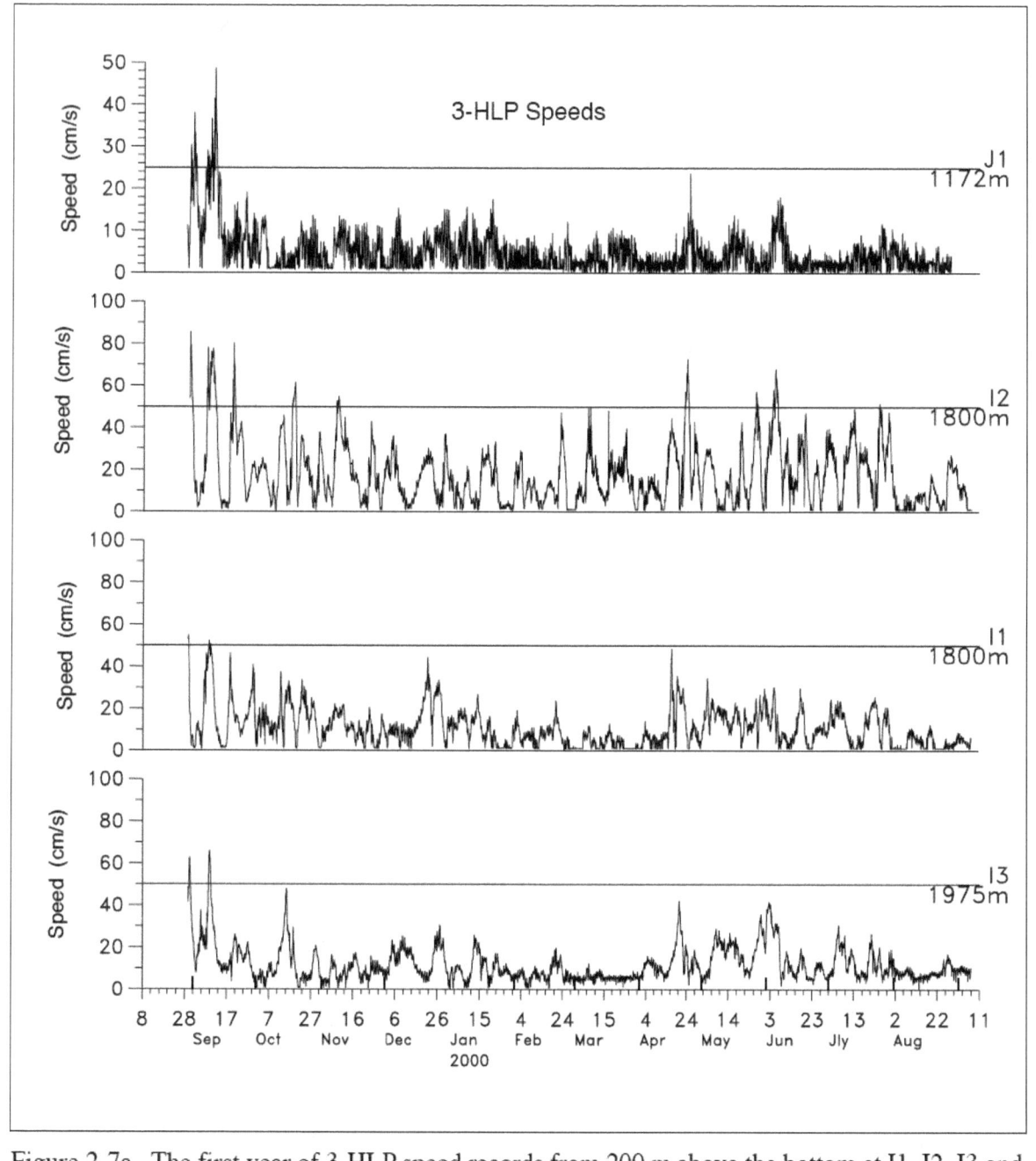

Figure 2-7a. The first year of 3-HLP speed records from 200 m above the bottom at I1, I2, I3 and J1. Note the change of velocity scale for J1.

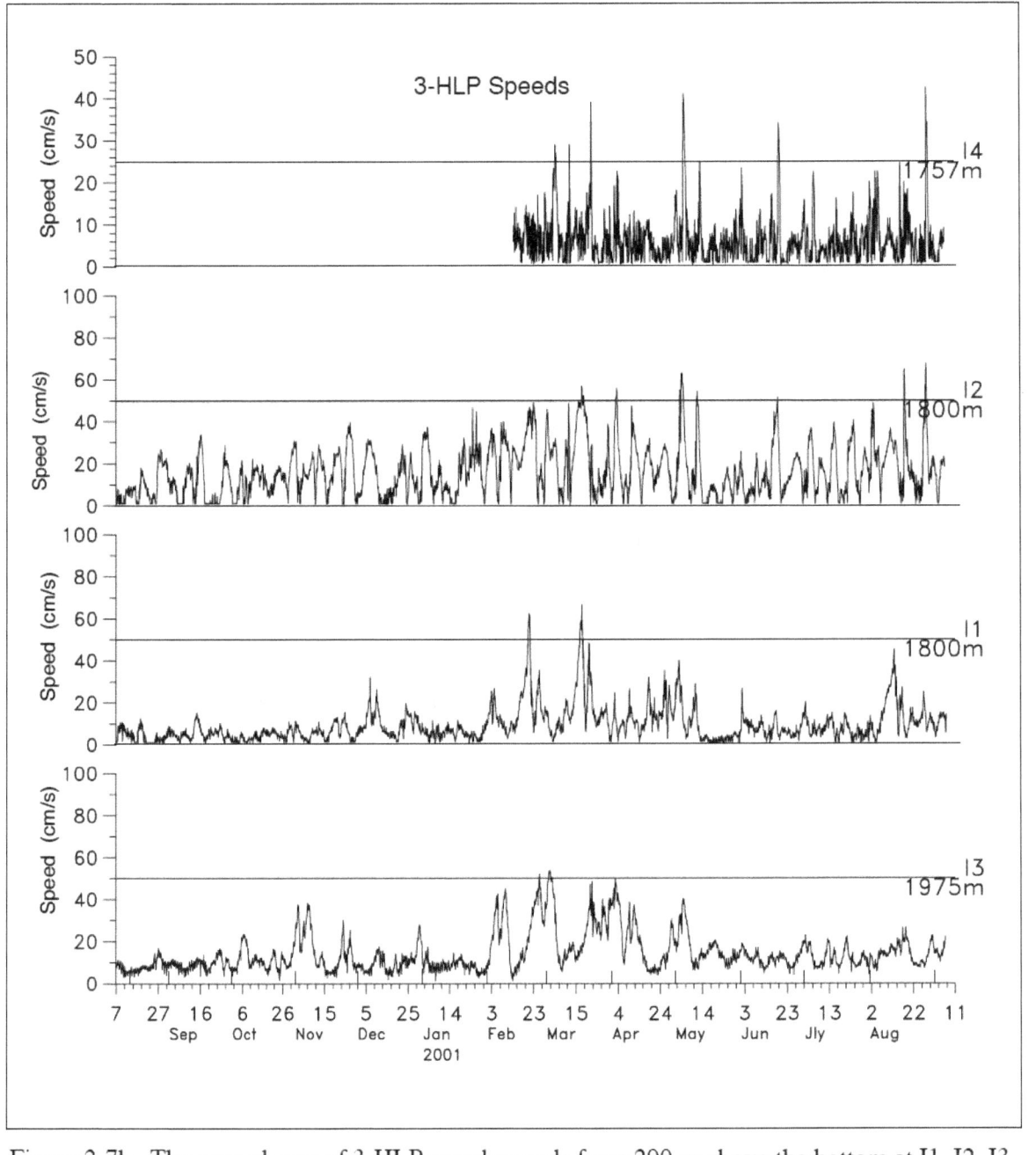

Figure 2-7b. The second year of 3-HLP speed records from 200 m above the bottom at I1, I2, I3 and I4. Note the change of velocity scale for I4.

27

3.0 ANALYSIS OF CURRENTS

3.1   Basic Statistics

The basic statistics for all current records below 1000 m, and selected records from the upper-layer at I1, are given in Table 3-1. The means, standard deviations and extremes are given for the 3-HLP east and north components and speeds. The standard deviations are also given for the 40-HLP velocities along with the ratio between the 40 and 3-HLP kinetic energy, and principal axis directions. The latter are calculated with the 40-HLP data and the ratio shows how the degree the low frequency motions dominate the variances of each record. In the lower layer (normally below 1000 m water depth), the maximum standard deviations and speeds are found at the I2 mooring followed by I3, I1, J1 and I4 in decreasing order. However, I4 and J1 are very similar and the higher speeds observed at J1 were caused by the initial September event when maximum speeds at J1 were comparable to I1 (~ 50 cm/s). This first strong event in the record also produced the 95 cm/s maximum speed at I2. If you exclude the first two weeks of the record at J1, then the maximum speed observed at 1361 m was 29.2 cm/s which is smaller than the maximum speeds measured at I4. It is noted that all the near-bottom instruments, which were in the frictional boundary layer, show a 10° anticlockwise rotation of the principal axis compared to the instrument 200 m from the bottom. This is consistent with Ekman turning in the bottom boundary layer.

A summary of the low-frequency variance of the deep current data is given in Figure 3-1 in the form of standard deviation ellipses. The amplification of the KE from I1 to I2 on the same isobath, separated by only 23 km is clearly evident. The variance at I3 is similar to I1, but is less polarized with the major axis being at an angle to the isobaths. Motions at J1, above the escarpment and 30 km from I2, and I4, only 6 km west of I2, however, had small variances compared to the I1, I2, and I3 moorings. Therefore, the steep slope of the escarpment appears to have insulated the region to the west and north from the energetic deep water motions. The ellipses at 200 m and 1000 m from the bottom are shown for I1, and clearly demonstrate the bottom trapped nature of the current fluctuations. Mean currents are also given in Figure 3-1 for the two-year 40-HLP records. There was a small mean southwestward current at I3, but at the base of the escarpment (I1 and I2) the means were of order 5 cm/s at 200-m from the bottom. Smaller mean flows were observed at I4 and J1 for shorter averaging periods. Again, it is unknown if the escarpment slope had a role in generating a moderate westward near-bottom mean current that again had considerable variation over the short distances between I3 and J1.

In the upper layer at I1, means, maxima and standard deviations decreased with depth. This is mainly the influence of the two major LC eddies that were over the measurement site for approximately 9 months out of the 24 months. The minimum in the statistics of the whole water column at I1 occurred at 1000 m and illustrates the two-layer nature of the deep Gulf. Energy in the currents increased both above and below this level with the maxima occurring near the water column boundaries (i.e. surface and bottom).

Table 3-1. Statistics of currents measured during this project. The first column shows the mooring ID and the depth below the surface of the measured current time series. Positive U is east; positive V is north. All velocities and speeds are in cm/s.

Depth (m)	Mean (3-HLP) U	V	Speed	Std Dev (3-HLP) U	V	Speed	Maximum (3-HLP) U	V	Speed	Minimum (3-HLP) U	V	% of Time with Records	Std Dev (40-HLP) U	V	Speed	Ratio 40-HLP:3-HLP Kinetic Energy (%)	Principal Axis Direction (Degrees True)
I1	Time Period: 8/29/1999 - 9/06/2001			Coordinate Rotation 0						Water Depth: 2000 m							
32	12.00	7.02	44.04	37.03	29.84	29.14	139.6	154.8	154.8	-113.0	-112.0	83	36.40	28.79	28.50	95	103
106	15.63	0.47	35.95	30.72	28.33	26.24	118.1	98.5	123.7	-72.6	-106.6	100	30.36	27.57	25.71	96	127
198	7.54	0.76	22.04	20.34	18.31	17.72	76.3	71.0	83.7	-55.7	-68.1	100	20.06	17.66	17.29	95	125
300	5.35	0.32	18.02	16.11	15.08	13.66	69.1	53.6	74.3	-49.5	-55.7	100	15.77	14.50	13.19	94	129
410	4.72	-0.45	15.33	16.10	11.31	13.08	59.9	49.6	60.0	-46.5	-41.1	46	15.53	10.74	12.61	92	113
588/602	4.04	1.56	12.08	10.75	9.34	8.32	45.8	34.5	47.3	-36.7	-26.1	51	10.24	8.49	7.64	78	94
802	0.48	-0.21	7.40	7.28	5.33	5.11	30.7	20.1	47.6	-45.0	-25.3	100	6.50	4.32	4.29	75	89
1000	-0.80	0.03	6.01	6.46	4.15	4.76	27.5	20.0	40.3	-38.8	-19.1	100	6.01	3.77	4.21	85	71
1200	-1.12	0.20	7.31	8.59	5.33	6.96	34.6	31.8	49.7	-49.3	-30.9	81	8.19	4.96	6.50	90	64
1400	-1.49	0.15	8.87	9.66	6.48	7.58	42.2	32.6	53.4	-52.9	-37.0	94	9.46	6.27	7.36	95	62
1600	-2.74	0.96	9.01	10.16	6.11	8.22	42.8	30.8	52.3	-52.1	-43.6	72	9.92	5.87	7.93	95	66
1800	-2.76	1.31	10.30	11.07	7.05	8.64	54.9	38.3	66.3	-53.9	-44.1	100	10.85	6.82	8.39	95	64
I2	Time Period: 8/29/1999 - 9/06/2001			Coordinate Rotation 0						Water Depth 1998 m							
1979	-1.43	0.78	10.64	11.27	8.88	9.72	50.2	49.5	67.5	-36.7	-47.3	50	11.08	8.60	9.55	96	56
1800	-4.09	-0.91	16.75	16.88	8.05	9.15	40.9	21.5	90.1	-76.9	-58.6	100	16.46	7.49	8.62	94	67
1600	-4.53	0.39	17.15	20.27	6.60	13.31	49.9	30.2	85.6	-72.5	-49.6	100	19.91	6.21	12.84	96	76
1600	-4.73	0.37	16.97	19.54	6.08	12.13	47.7	23.5	95.0	-95.0	-29.0	73	19.15	5.76	11.58	96	76
I3	Time Period: 8/29/1999 - 9/06/2001			Coordinate Rotation 0						Water Depth 1158 m							
1989	-0.91		16.88														
1775	-0.97	-0.44	13.09	14.42	9.04	10.46	50.2	43.3	73.7	-72.5	-41.9	68	14.07	8.80	10.07	93	104
1975	-1.00	-0.94	13.33	13.64	8.58	9.00	47.2	39.5	66.1	-65.0	-40.1	100	13.31	8.34	8.69	95	103
2164	-1.28	-1.45	12.79	13.69	7.75	9.22	48.6	22.5	68.1	-59.1	-46.0	100	13.37	7.58	8.91	96	89
J1	Time Period: 8/28/1999 - 8/28/2000			Coordinate Rotation 0						Water Depth 1373 m							
972	-1.20	-0.53	5.07	5.38	3.45	4.07	21.6	10.8	36.6	-36.5	-24.7	100	4.60	2.33	3.38	65	81
1172	-2.00	-0.56	4.88	4.99	3.13	4.99	15.1	16.4	48.8	-48.7	-27.1	100	5.27	2.04	4.38	72	89
1361	-4.34	0.00	6.54	6.84	4.38	6.43	12.2	22.7	49.5	-47.1	-24.4	88	5.87	3.20	5.57	68	67
I4	Time Period: 2/13/2001 - 9/06/2001			Coordinate Rotation 0						Water Depth 1957 m							
1557	-0.90	0.71	7.43	7.74	3.75	4.32	22.6	19.2	30.2	-29.3	-12.3	28	7.23	2.89	3.75	82	78
1757	-1.86	0.74	6.44	7.63	3.49	5.68	15.0	15.5	42.5	-41.7	-11.6	28	6.87	2.69	5.00	77	94

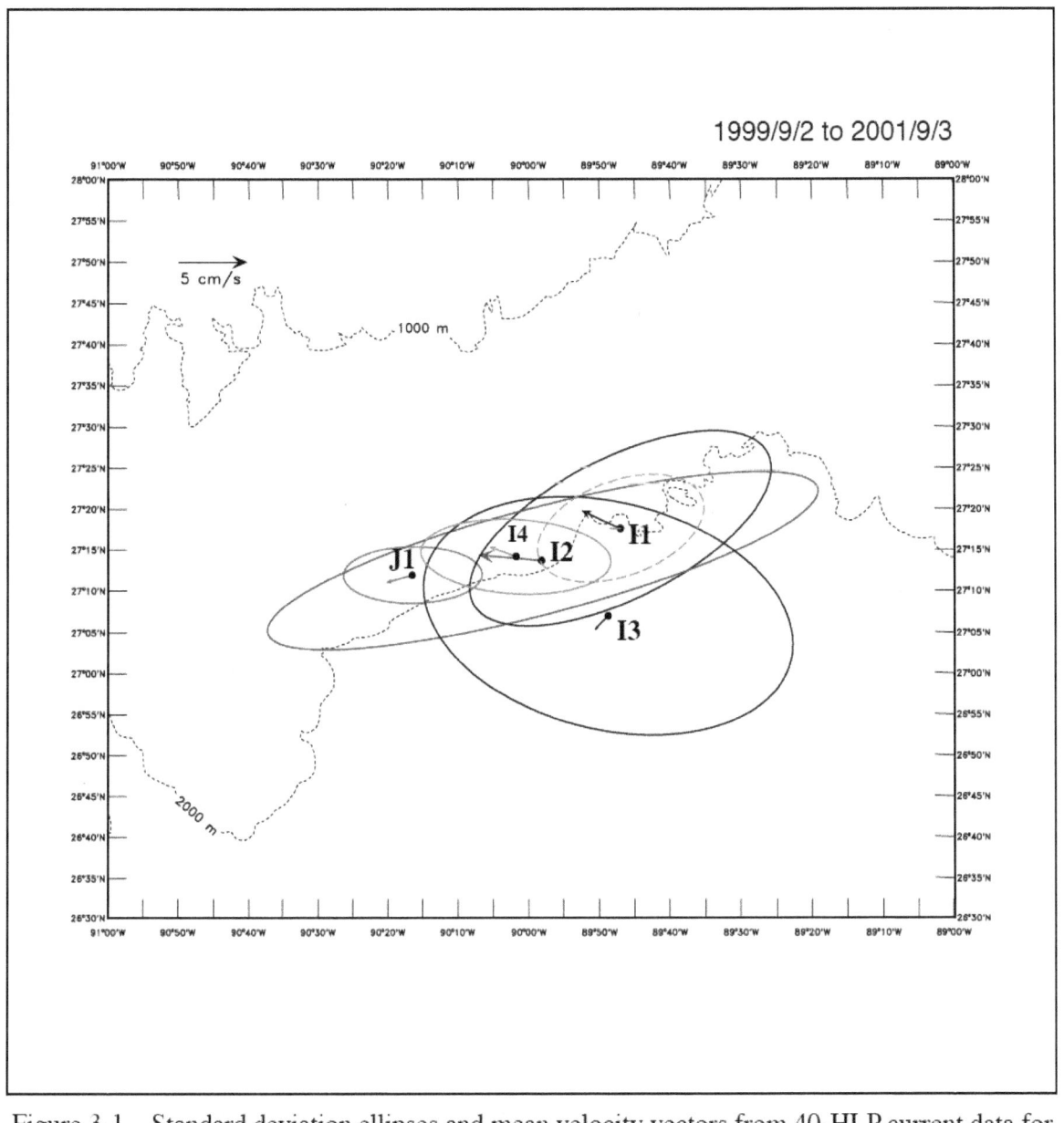

Figure 3-1. Standard deviation ellipses and mean velocity vectors from 40-HLP current data for 200 m and 1000 m (green and dashed) above the bottom. Two-year long records used except for J1 (12 months - magenta) and I4 (6 months - red). Only I1 provided measurements 1000 m above the bottom.

3.2   Topographic Rossby Waves

The basic description of the lower-layer currents in Chapter 2 emphasized the wave-like nature of the nearly barotropic fluctuations in the lower 1000 m of the water column. Rhines (1970) first gave the theory of topographic Rossby waves. Important features of TRW theory are:

1. The wave motion is bottom intensified; thus current amplitudes increase in magnitude towards the bottom.

2. There is no phase difference between currents at different depths; therefore at any particular wave frequency, the motion is columnar.

3. The maximum frequency or cutoff frequency for TRW's is $N\alpha$ where α is the bottom slope, defined as normal to the general trend of the isobaths, and N is the Brunt-Vaisala frequency of the lower water column. Bottom slopes are defined over scales similar to the wavelengths of TRW's (~ 50 to 100 km). The effect of small or large perturbations of the bottom slope on TRW propagation is not covered by present linear theories. The wave frequency, ω, is proportional to the bottom slope and the cosine of the angle that the wavevector makes with the isobaths. At the highest allowed frequency, the phase velocity is parallel to the isobaths such that shallow water is on the right of the direction of wave propagation.

4. At the highest allowed frequency, wave motions are rectilinear and perpendicular to the phase vector and isobaths. At lower frequencies the wave motions become more parallel to the isobaths. Longer wave-length motions are also less bottom trapped than high frequency waves.

5. TRW's are dispersive and it can be shown that if the phase vector is directed into deeper water, then the energy flux has component towards the shallower water (Thompson, 1977). TRW's are refracted by changing topography. These ray-paths can be calculated by WKB theory which assumes that the environment (e.g. bottom slopes) change "slowly" compared to the wavelength of the motions. This is rarely strictly true in practice.

TRW ray paths in this study were calculated using the full dispersion relation. The basis of the method is given in Meinen et al. (1993b) and used by Pickart (1995) to calculate TRW ray paths generated by the deep Gulf Stream in the Middle Atlantic Bight. The dispersion relation for TRW's is given by the coupled equations (Pickart, 1995):

$$\lambda^2 = (k^2 + l^2 + \beta k/\omega)(N/f)^2 \tag{1}$$

$$\lambda \tanh(\lambda h) = N^2/(\omega f)(kh_y - lh_x) \tag{2}$$

where   h is the water depth,
                 N is the constant Brunt-Väisälä frequency,
                 f is the Coriolis parameter using the β-plane assumption,
                 $\mathbf{k} = (k, l)$ is the wavenumber vector in east and north (x, y) coordinates,
                 ω is the wave frequency, and
                 $1/\lambda$ is the vertical trapping scale of the wave.

Under the WKB approximation, where changes in wave amplitude and phase caused by the environment are assumed to vary on scales larger than the local wavelength, the equations governing the path of a wave and its wavenumber are (LeBlond and Mysak, 1978):

$$D_t \mathbf{x} = \partial \omega / \partial \mathbf{k} = \mathbf{c_g} \qquad (3)$$

$$D_t \mathbf{k} = \sum - \partial \omega / \partial \gamma_i \nabla \gamma_i \qquad (4)$$

where $\quad D_t = \partial / \partial t + \mathbf{c_g} \bullet \nabla$

is the derivative following the wavegroup, $\mathbf{x}$ is the path of the ray, and $\mathbf{c_g}$ is the group velocity. The γ_I are the environmental parameters that cause refraction of the wave. There are three such parameters for TRWs: h (water depth), ∇h (bottom slope), and N (Brunt-Väisälä frequency). N is assumed constant for these calculations. The WKB assumption is marginal though it is often used under conditions that have sharp changes in the environmental parameters. Therefore, the topography must be smoothed over at least the wavelength scale for the method to apply. This is discussed in Section 3.6. The ray tracing equations, (3) and (4), are solved using 4th order Runge-Kutta methods to determine ray paths, and the change in the wavenumbers along the rays. Essentially the same method was used by Oey and Lee (2002) for an investigation of TRWs generated by a numerical circulation model of the Gulf of Mexico basin.

3.3 Spectra

The kinetic energy (KE) spectra, in variance preserving form, i.e. equal areas under the curve represent equal contributions to the variances, were calculated for lower-layer instruments. Because there were differences between the various wave trains observed in the lower layer records, KE spectra were calculated for five periods of 100 to 120 days that included the events discussed in the previous section. Table 3-2 summarizes these periods and includes the complete two-year period that is used for analysis of longer period motions.

The KE spectra for the currents, 200 m from the bottom are given in Figure 3-2. The two-year spectra show the dominance of the motions at I2 over the frequency band 0.02 to 0.09 cpd (50 to 11 day periods). At periods shorter than 8 days, the spectra at the three I instruments are similar. Between 8 and 11 days, I1 had about half the KE of I2 and I3. The maximum energy difference between I2 and its neighbors occurred at periods of about 16 to 20 days. The spectral peak at 16 to 20 days and the lack of energy at periods longer than about 30 to 40 days are similar to spectra of deep currents in the western and central Gulf (Hamilton, 1990). In the eastern Gulf, under the LC, spectra did show high energy at 20 to 25 days, but also at longer periods (Hamilton and Lugo-Fernandez, 2001). The difference between the spectra for this site (Figure 3-2) and other regions of the Gulf is the high-energy peak at 8 to 11 day periods. The lack of energy at periods shorter than about 5 to 7 days corresponds to the cut-off frequency for TRWs that depends on bottom slope and lower-layer stratification.

Table 3-2. Spectra and TRW Analysis Periods

Period	Start Date (yyyy-mm-dd)	Length (days)	Upper-Layer Circulations
1	1999-09-03	100	Eddy J
2	1999-12-01	100	Cyclones on J
3	2000-04-01	120	Eddy K (weak anticyclone)
4	2000-09-02	120	Cyclones
5	2001-02-19	120	Eddy M
Two-Year	1999-09-03	730	Complete Observation Period

The spectra, for the September to December, 1999 interval (Period 1, Figure 3-2), show that the dominant response at I1 and I2 was at about the 8 – 9 day period. Both I1 and I2 were amplified over the broadband red spectra at I3. The energy at J1, which was above the escarpment, was negligible compared to the I moorings, as it is for all the periods where comparisons can be made (Figure 3-2). The second period has about a 10-day overlap with period 1, but even so the spectral peaks show a shift to a lower frequencies, with periods of 11 to 12 days. Energy levels were much lower because this period includes February and March 2000, which was relatively quiescent. However, I1 and I2 were still elevated above I3. In the April to August period (3), the spectral peak shifted to 12- to 15-day periods with relatively little energy at periods shorter than 10 days. The amplification of I2 over I1 and I3, which had similar energy levels, was larger than in the earlier periods. In period 4, another interval of relatively low energy, the characteristic peak remained at about 14 days, but I3 had similar variances to period 3 and both I1 and I2 diminished considerably. I2, however, still had the largest variances. For the last wave train that begins in February 2001 (period 5), there was a distinct change in characteristics. Unlike all the previous periods, I2 did not have the highest energy levels over most of the energetic frequencies. I3 dominated and there were two spectral peaks, at about 8 days, and 17 to 20 days, respectively. The energy levels at I4 were much smaller than at the other three moorings, with most of its energy at shorter periods than 10 days.

These results imply that the wave trains, which can be identified in Figures 2-5 and 2-6, had distinctly different characteristics with different dominant periods and horizontal distributions of KE. These differences between wave trains suggest that they may have had different origins. KE spectra calculated for the BP mooring, which was within a few kilometers of I1, showed that fluctuations at 7- to 10-day periods dominated the September 1997 to April 1998 measurement period (Hamilton, 1998). 16-day motions were present at a spectral peak, but with lesser amplitudes. The two-year KE spectra in Figure 3-2 are an indication of "average" conditions and indicate there were two dominant periods, around 8 to 12 days and 16 to 20 days. The shorter periods dominated at I3, which had similar energy levels to I2, and the longer periods at I2 and I1. I2 had two to three times the variance of I1 and I3 at this longer period. The records at J1 and I4 show that this high energy only intermittently penetrated west and upslope of I2. This

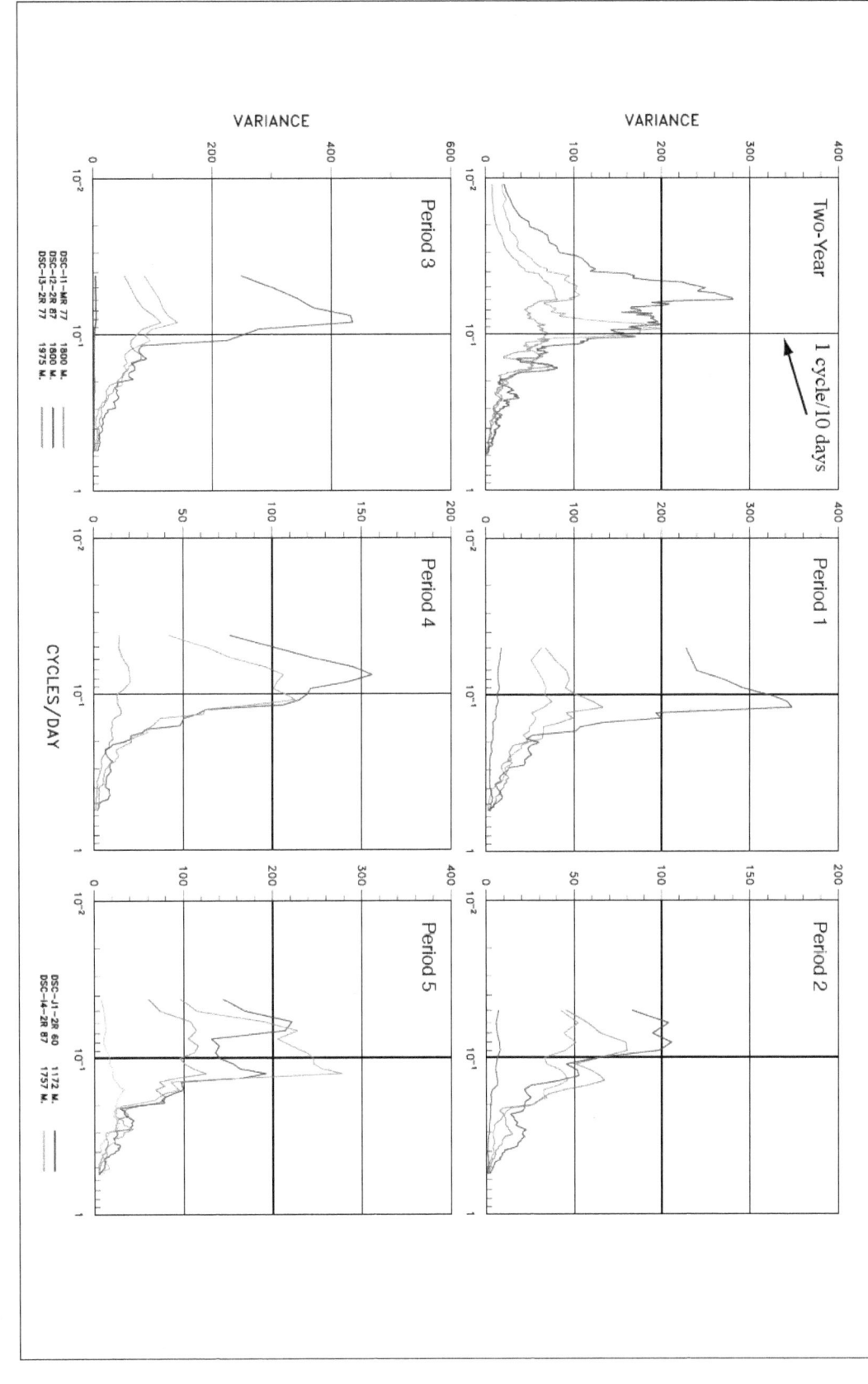

Figure 3-2. Kinetic energy spectra in variance preserving form, for 40-HLP velocities from instruments 200-m above the bottom, for moorings I1, I2, I3, J1 and I4 (see color code). The analysis periods are given in Table 3-2. Degrees of freedom are 30 and 18 for the two-year and period calculations, respectively.

spatial inhomogeneity implies, perhaps, that topography was strongly influencing the TRW wave trains through focusing and reflection of energy; there was non-linear transfer of energy between frequency bands; and/or that this could have been a genesis region.

It is useful to examine how the motions at 200 m from the bottom decay with increasing distance above the seabed. Figure 3-3 shows the KE spectra at the 1000, 1400 and 1800-m levels of I1 for the intervals defined in Table 3-2. The two-year spectra are split, approximately equally, between the 7 to 12 day and 12 to 30 day period bands. Both bands show decay with height with the shorter periods showing less penetration to the 1000-m level than the longer periods. This is in agreement with TRW theory as shorter period, and therefore, shorter wavelength TRW's are more strongly bottom trapped. However, spectra during period 1, 2 and 4 show that motions were nearly depth-independent when the 1400 and 1800-m levels are compared. Spectra for periods 3 and 5, on the other hand, show strong decay with height above the bottom for periods longer than 7-days. This, again, implies that the wave trains had different characteristics at different periods and thus, could have been generated by very different processes. Hogg (2000) also found strongly bottom intensified and nearly barotropic motions in the same region of the tail of the Grand Banks.

3.4   Vertical EOF Analysis at I1

The spectra for I1 (Figure 3-3) were used for frequency domain EOF analyses of the depth dependence of the energetic currents. The resulting structures of the coherent motions in the lower water column are given in Figure 3-4 where the frequency bands are centered on the spectral peak of each of the analysis periods. Only one frequency band was used for each interval except period 5 where the high and low frequency peaks were about equal. The first mode, in all cases, accounted for a very high percentage (85 to 95%) of the total variance of both the U and V-components at the available instrumented levels below 1000 m. The exception is the quiescent period 4 where the relatively weak fluctuations accounted for 72% of the total variance of the 6 depths used for this analysis. This is consistent with the fluctuations being dominated by highly coherent TRWs. The fluctuations were also in-phase through the water column and all the modes show a decrease in amplitude with height above the bottom. Themajor axes of the fluctuations were aligned approximately with the general trend of the isobaths. In period 5, the longer period motions were rotated anticlockwise from the shorter period fluctuations, and thus the former had a larger cross-isobath component. This is a departure from linear TRW theory in that it is expected that the major axes of shorter period motions should be more perpendicular to the isobaths than the longer period motions. This inconsistency will be discussed further when the horizontal structure of the waves is presented. Otherwise the longer period band showed less decay with height than the shorter which implies a smaller trapping depth with higher frequency. This is the behavior expected from the theory.

The periods (1, 3 and 5) with major events had similar energy levels but different degrees of bottom intensification. Periods 1 and 2 had almost uniform motion at the bottom three levels (1400, 1600 and 1800 m) with decrease in amplitudes only observed at the two levels above these. The short period motions in periods 3 and 5 had a marked decay with height above the bottom. Period 3 peak frequency was lower than period 1, which should favor more barotropic fluctuations rather than the opposite. This further confirms that the different wave trains had

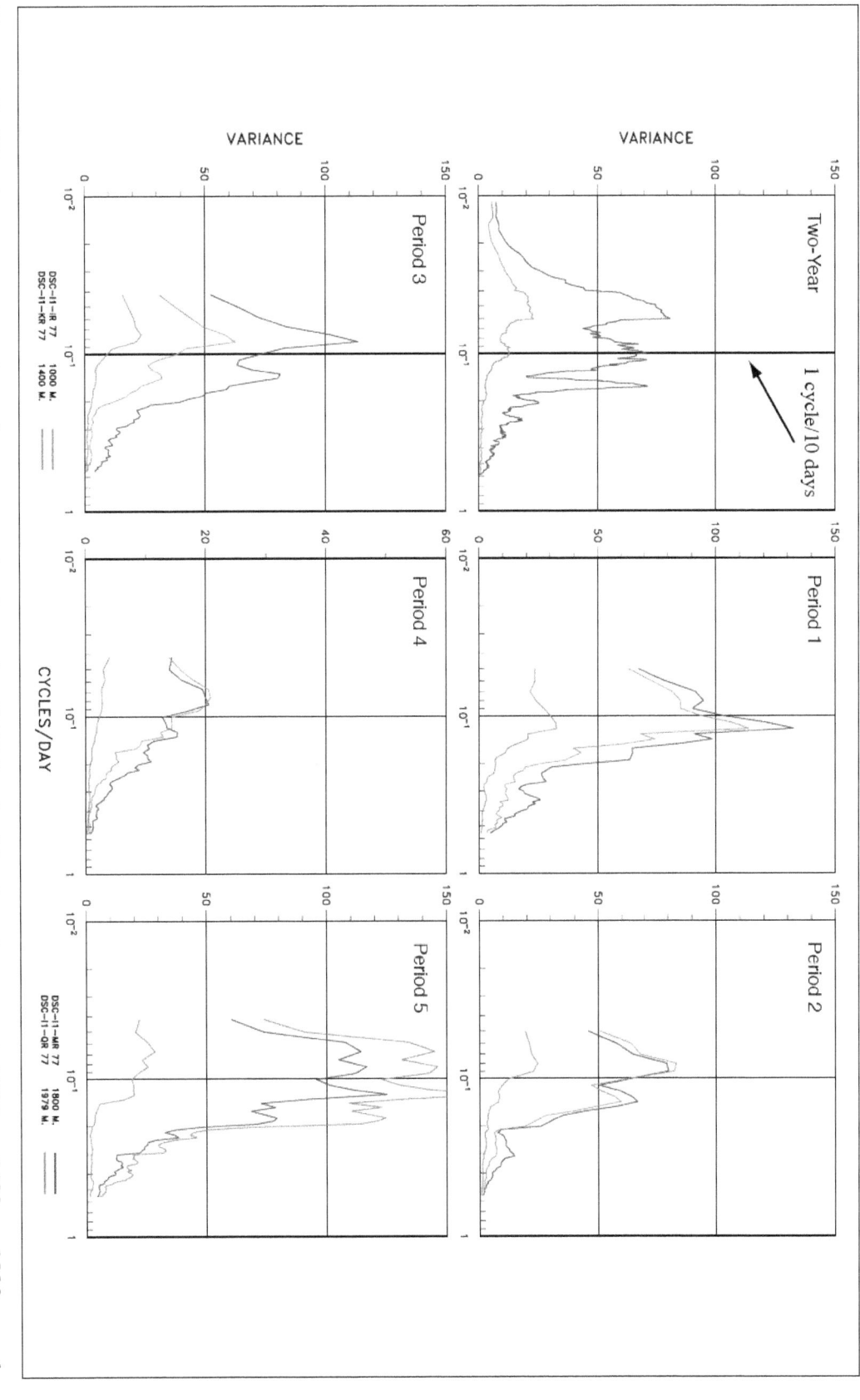

Figure 3-3. Kinetic energy spectra in variance preserving form, for 40-HLP velocities from instruments 1000-m, 1400-m, 1800-m and 1979-m (Period 5 only) depths, for mooring II (see color code). The analysis periods are given in Table 3-2. Degrees of freedom are 30 and 18 for the two-year and period calculations, respectively.

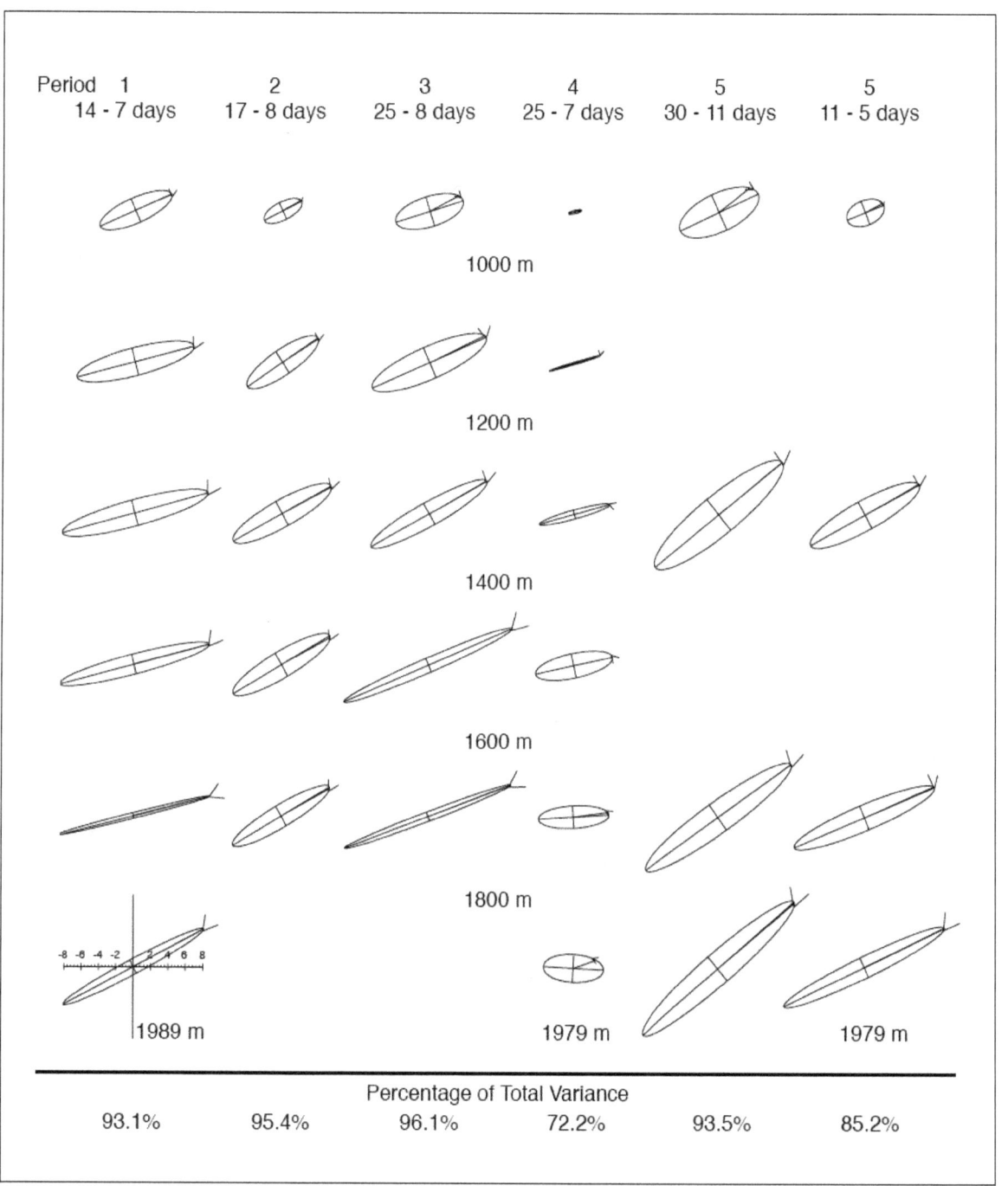

Figure 3-4. Mode 1, represented as hodographs, resulting from EOF analyses of current records at I1 below 1000 m for the indicated periods (see Table 3-2) and frequency bands.

38

different characteristics, and thus, may not have been generated by exactly the same processes. During period 3, the wave train occurred when the surface layer currents were small and is of interest to determine how far into the surface layer, bottom trapped TRWs can be traced. The other events occurred when energetic LC eddies were present and any TRW signal above 800 to 1000 m would be overwhelmed by the eddy currents. Figure 3-5 shows the hodographs for period 3, using records fairly equally spaced with depth through the water column. The signal was significantly coherent with the mode at all levels below 300 m. The upper 3 levels can probably be regarded as being primarily noise. The second mode (not shown) accounted for 15% of the total variance and was surface intensified with only the top 4 levels being significant. Therefore, in this period, when the surface circulation was dominated by a weak anticyclone (Eddy K), strong TRW motions accounted for the majority (73%) of the energy in the 2000-m water column at I1. This is interesting because TRW theory (Rhines, 1970) indicates that such wave motions involve the whole water column, but this has not been previously observed to the author's knowledge, except during a similar quiescent period at the BP Atwater mooring (Hamilton, 1998).

The trapping depths can be found by least-square fitting of the major axis amplitudes to the function $A_0 \cosh(\lambda z)$ where the depth z is measured upwards from the ocean surface (depth below the sea surface is negative) and $(1/\lambda)$ is the trapping depth. The wavelength of the TRW's is then related to λ by equation (1) with $\beta = 0$, i.e.

$$\lambda = NK/f$$

where $K = (k^2 + l^2)^{1/2}$ is the wavenumber magnitude and f, the Coriolis parameter (= 6.67 10^{-5} s^{-1}). The resulting trapping depths and wavelengths (= $2\pi/K$) for the six profiles, shown in Figure 3-4, are given in Table 3-3.

Table 3-3. TRW Wave Parameters

Analysis Period	Frequency Band (days)	Trapping Depth (m)	Wavelength (km)	Wavelength and Direction from Horizontal EOFs	
1	14-7	1588	151	76	180°T
2	17-8	893	85	50	189°T
3	25-8	896	85	62	188°T
4	25-7	793	75	70	198°T
5	30-11	1237	118	87	191°T
5	11-5	683	65	73	191°T
Two-year	30-15	-	-	68	187°T
Two-year	15-7	-	-	68	194°T

39

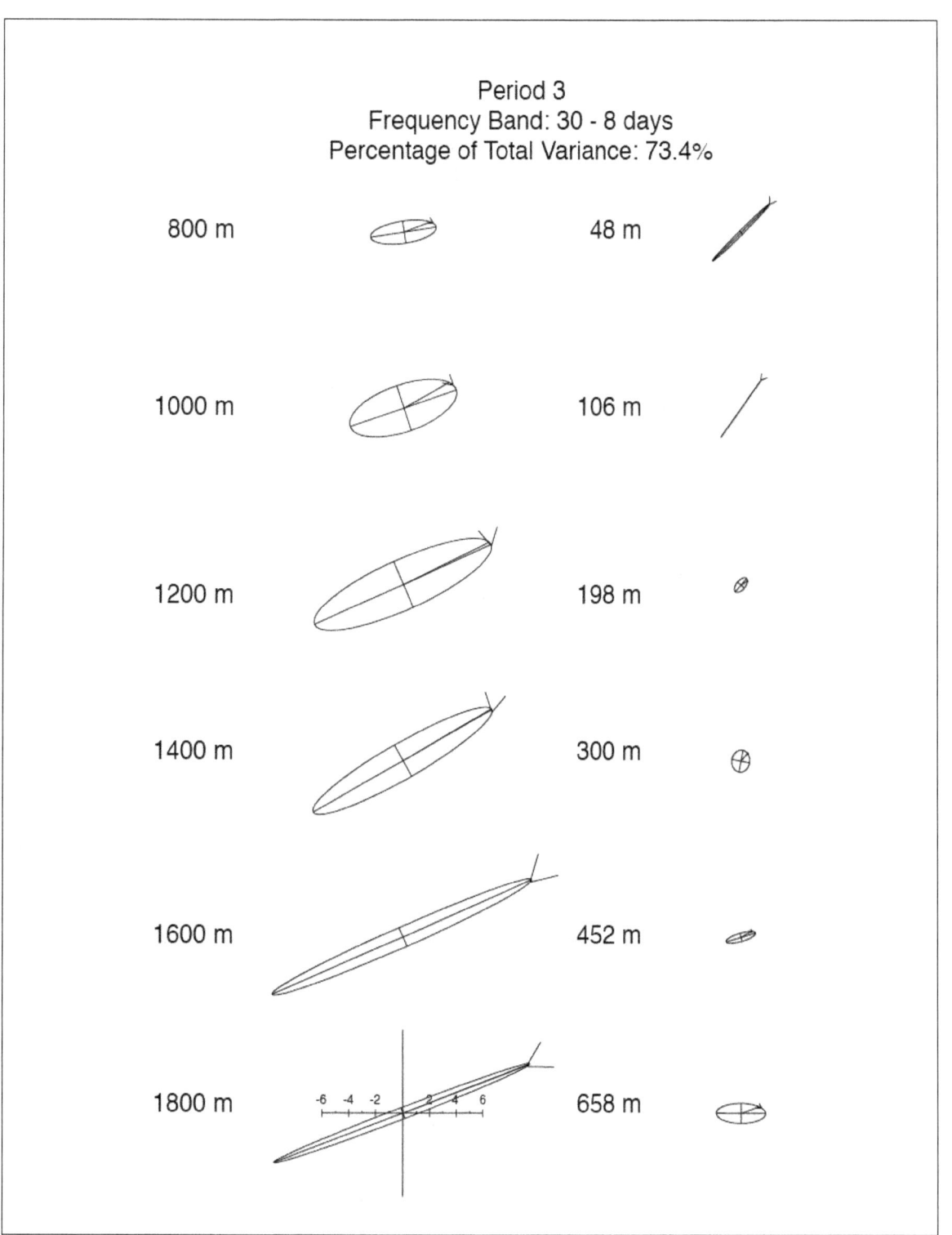

Figure 3-5. Mode 1, represented as hodographs, resulting from EOF analyses of current records at I1 for the complete water column. Analysis period 3 (April - August, 2000) when surface layer currents are weak.

Table 3-3 shows that trapping depth decreased with shorter periods for the period 5 EOF analysis, and the period 1 was less bottom trapped than the later periods. The inferred wavelengths are short and range from 60 to 150 km.

3.5 Horizontal EOF Analysis

The investigation of how the TRW motions varied in space used the records measured 200 m from the bottom at all of the moorings. The same frequency bands and periods were used as for the vertical analysis at I1. The results from the EOF analyses are given in Figure 3-6. The first modes dominate for all periods and exceed 76% of the total variances of the velocity records used. In the first year, the coherent responses at J1 were very small (amplitude ~ 1 cm/s) for all three wave trains. In the last six months, the coherent response at I4 (Figure 3-6c) was also small compared with the moorings to the east. The distribution of amplitudes across the main array (I1, I2 and I3) also varied with measurement period. Thus, maximum amplitudes were observed at I2 for periods 1, 3 and 4, I1 dominated for period 2, and I3 for period 5. Generally, I1 had less variance than I3, except for period 1. The phase relationships between the moorings were similar for all periods with I3 lagging I2 and I1, and I1 usually having a small lead over I2. The directions of the principal axes were consistent with this for the most part. Phase propagation was perpendicular to the principal axes such that the wavevector was directed into the 3rd or 4th quadrant in a isobath coordinate system with y normal to the trend of the isbaths and directed into shallow water. Usually the offshore propagation of phase (i.e. the wavevector directed into the 4th quadrant) is consistent with onshore propagation of wave energy from presumed deepwater generation regions. This was the case always for I3 and the principal axes of I2 were always nearly parallel to the escarpment. However, in period 2 (Figure 3-6a) and for the lower frequency waves in period 5, the wave vector at I1 (Figure 3-6c), the principal axis was rotated anticlockwise from the isobaths, implying onshore phase propagation. This may be an indication that the escarpment was reflecting some of the wave trains.

The differences between the directions of the major axes between frequency bands and between I3 and the records at the base of the escarpment are quite interesting. The major axis of I3 was at a distinct angle to the isobath and this angle usually increased, in a clockwise direction, as the period becomes shorter. Compare period 1 (Figure 3-6a) with period 3 (Figure 3-6b) and the low frequency variance ellipse for period 5 (Figure 3-6c). This is exactly how rectilinear fluctuations resulting from TRW's behave with increasing frequency. Therefore, it appears that the steep slope of the escarpment changes the direction of the water particle displacements causing the fluctuations to be along the slope and perhaps amplifying the signal as it propagated to the west. If the steep slope is considered to be a wall so that the cross-slope velocities are zero, then the TRW velocities are forced to be a long-slope, as observed. This would also imply that TRW energy would be reflected back into deep-water.

As a summary of average TRW characteristics, the two-year spectra were used to calculate the characteristic motions at 200 m from the bottom for I1, I2 and I3. The EOF analysis was divided into two frequency bands corresponding to the major peaks in the spectra (Figure 3-4). The energy at the 20- and 11-day periods was approximately the same and in both frequency bands, I1 and I2 had the maximum and minimum amplitudes, respectively. The phase relations were as

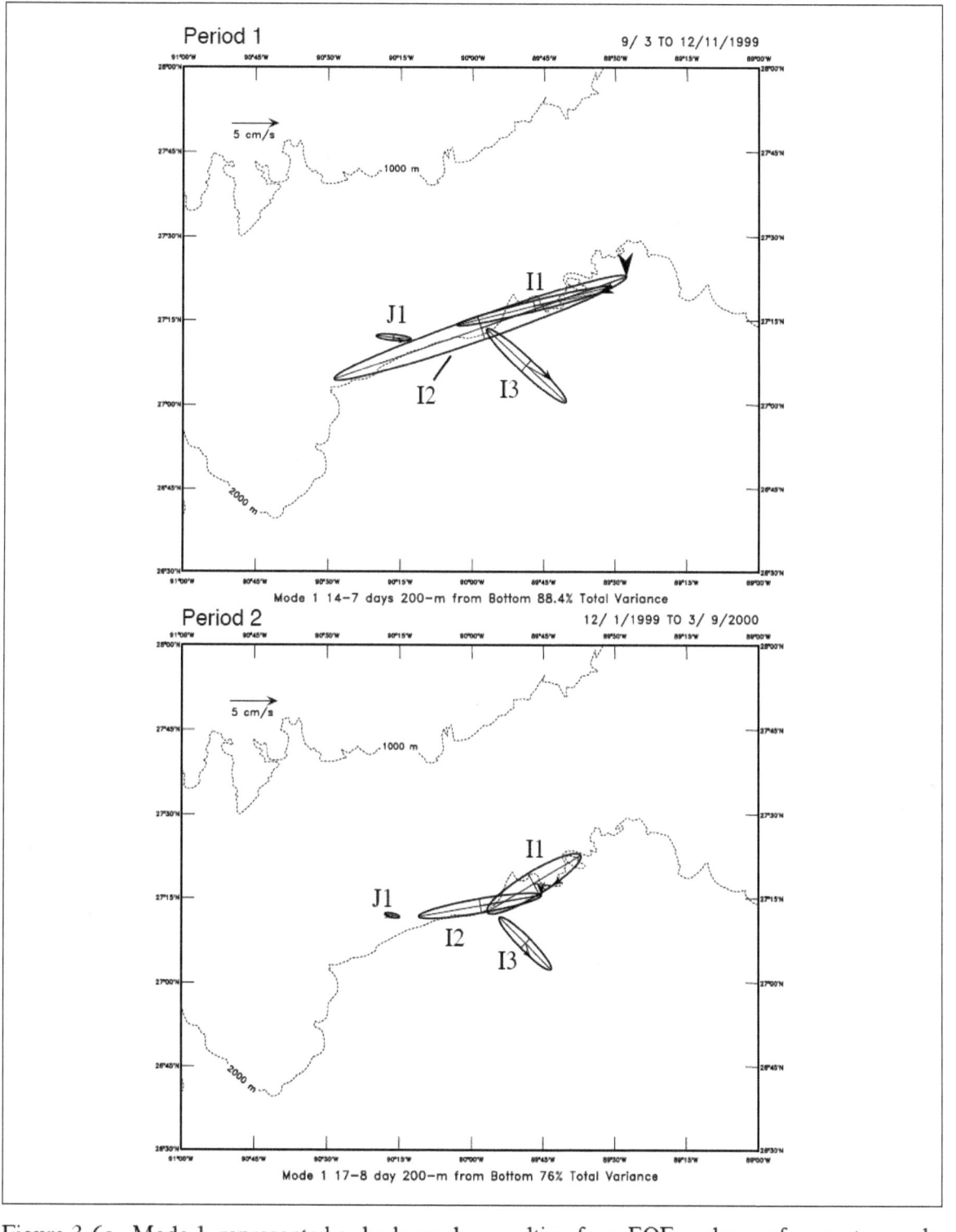

Figure 3-6a. Mode 1, represented as hodographs, resulting from EOF analyses of current records 200-m from the bottom for analysis periods 1 (14-7 days) and 2 (17-8 days).

42

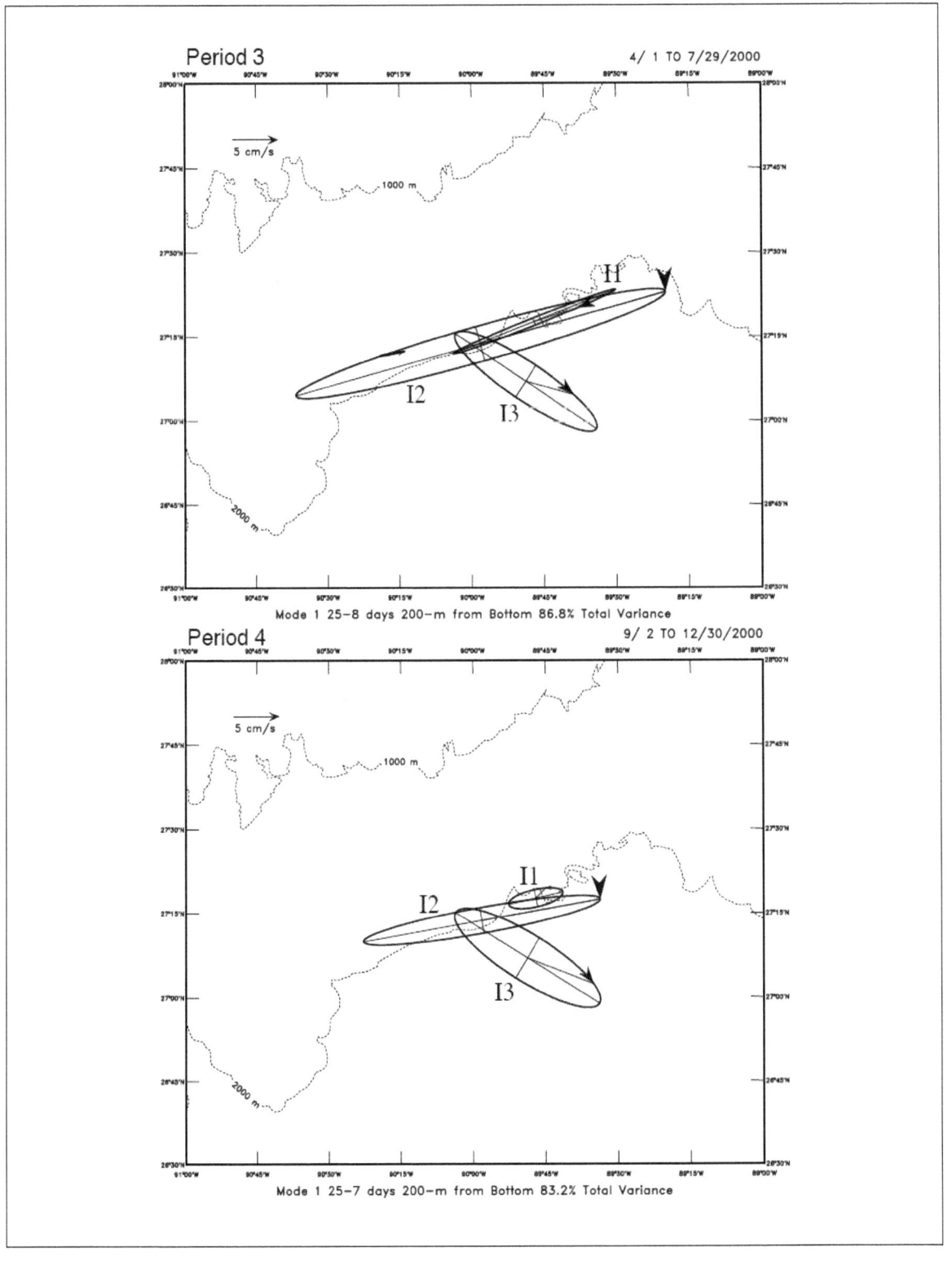

Figure 3-6b. Mode 1, represented as hodographs, resulting from EOF analyses of current records 200-m from the bottom for analysis periods 3 (25-8 days) and 4 (25-7 days).

43

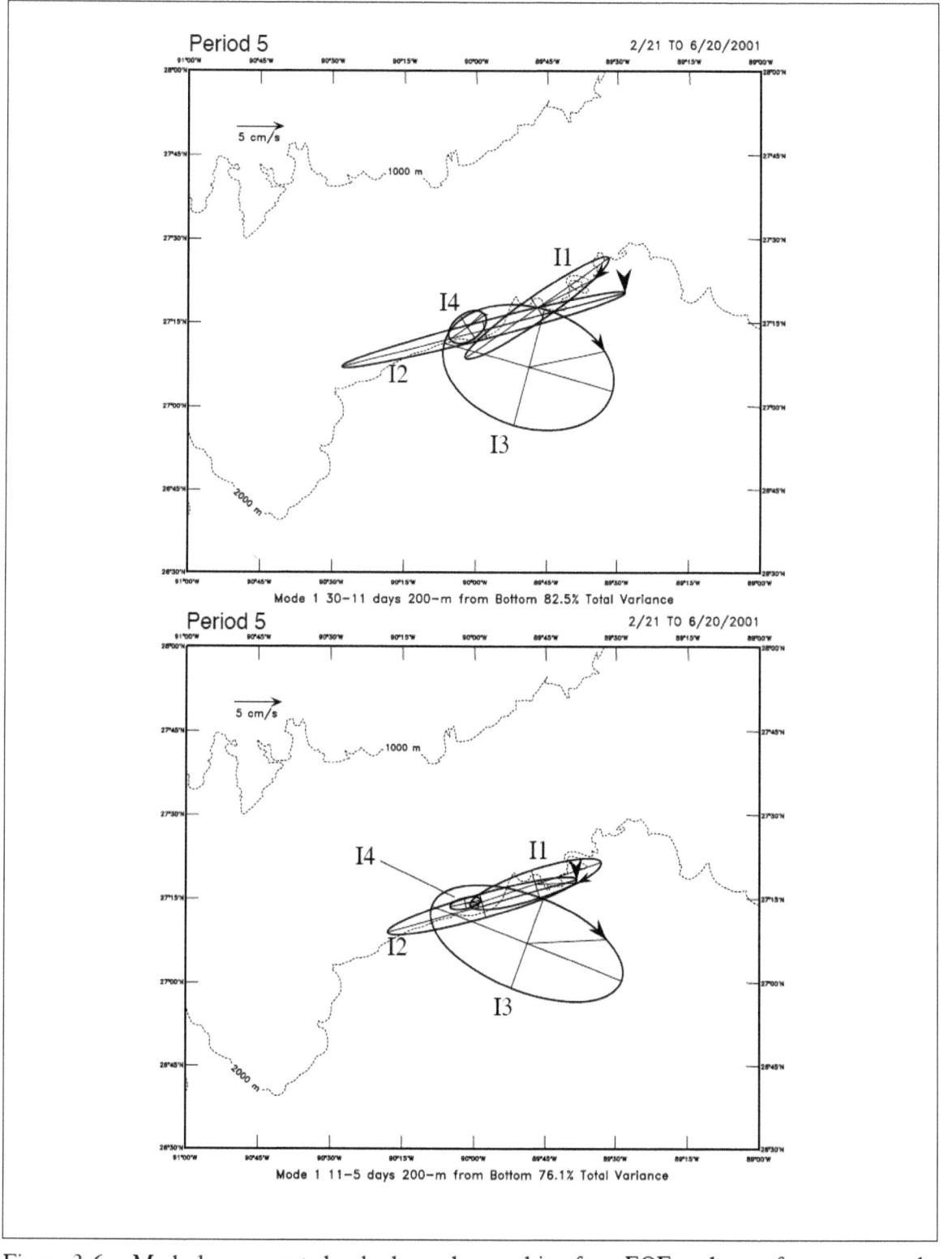

Figure 3-6c. Mode 1, represented as hodographs, resulting from EOF analyses of current records 200 m from the bottom for analysis period 5 using frequency bands 30-11 days (upper panel), and 11-5 days (lower panel).

given above and the principal axes of I1 and I3 rotated clockwise with increasing frequency (Figure 3-7).

The horizontal wavenumbers and their directions can be directly estimated by least squares fit from the phase differences between the moorings. These calculations were done without J1and I4 because of their low amplitudes compared to the other records. The results are given in the last column of Table 3-3 and are reasonably consistent with the wavelengths estimated from the trapping depths using the lower layer I1 records. Wavelengths of all cases were estimated to be between 50 and 90 km and the direction of phase propagation was south or slightly west of south. The two-year analysis suggests that 70 km is a reasonable value for the wavelength for both 20- and 11-day TRWs. This suggests similar source regions for the waves even though different period motions dominate at different times and their genesis may not be the same. The direction of phase propagation, calculated from the horizontal EOFs, was approximately perpendicular to mean direction of the major axes of the mooring data. This is an indication that estimating wave propagation direction from a single mooring may be misleading close to large topographic features.

3.6   TRW Ray Tracing

The WKB approximation assumes that the depth, h, and the bottom slope, ∇h, vary smoothly over length scales similar to the wavelength of the TRWs. For this study, the GTOPO 30 world ocean bathymetry data set was used as a starting point. Nominal resolutions are 2' of latitude and longitude. The northern slope region of the Gulf of Mexico has extremely rough bathymetry, so the challenge was to smooth the topography while keeping major features, such as the escarpment, but not introducing spurious features with surface fitting spline routines (e.g. oscillations where slopes have sharp changes). This was accomplished, after much experimentation, by first using a 50-km square median filter on the Gulf of Mexico subset of the bathymetry, and then fitting bivariate cubic smoothing splines to h and ∇h (Dierckx, 1982). The smoothing spline compromises between closeness-of-fit and smoothing by varying the number of knots over the grid. The resulting smoothed bathymetry is given in Figure 3-8.

The ray tracing equations (1-4) require initial conditions for the period and wavelength of the wave. Equations (3) and (4) were integrated forwards or backwards in time from the initial conditions to give an estimate of where the TRW has come from, and where it could propagate to, given the parameters at the measurement site. The integrations were terminated if the water becomes too shallow (i.e. no longer on the slope) or the group speed, c_g, becomes < 0.1 cm/s. For a given wavelength and period, the dispersion relation, (1) and (2), can be solved for the wavenumber components (k,l). If the bottom slope is aligned with l, then k is always negative, and there is a choice of sign for the upslope component of the wavenumber. For l directed up and down slope, the energy propagation has a component in the opposite direction and determines whether the wave propagates into deeper or shallower water, respectively. Thus, four ray paths can be traced from the starting point for a given period and initial wavelength. For each of the analysis periods, the TRW wave period was taken from the spectral peaks and the initial wavelengths from the results of the horizontal EOF analysis given in Table 3-3. These are given in Table 3-4, and the paths for the 20- and 8-day waves observed in period 5 are shown in

45

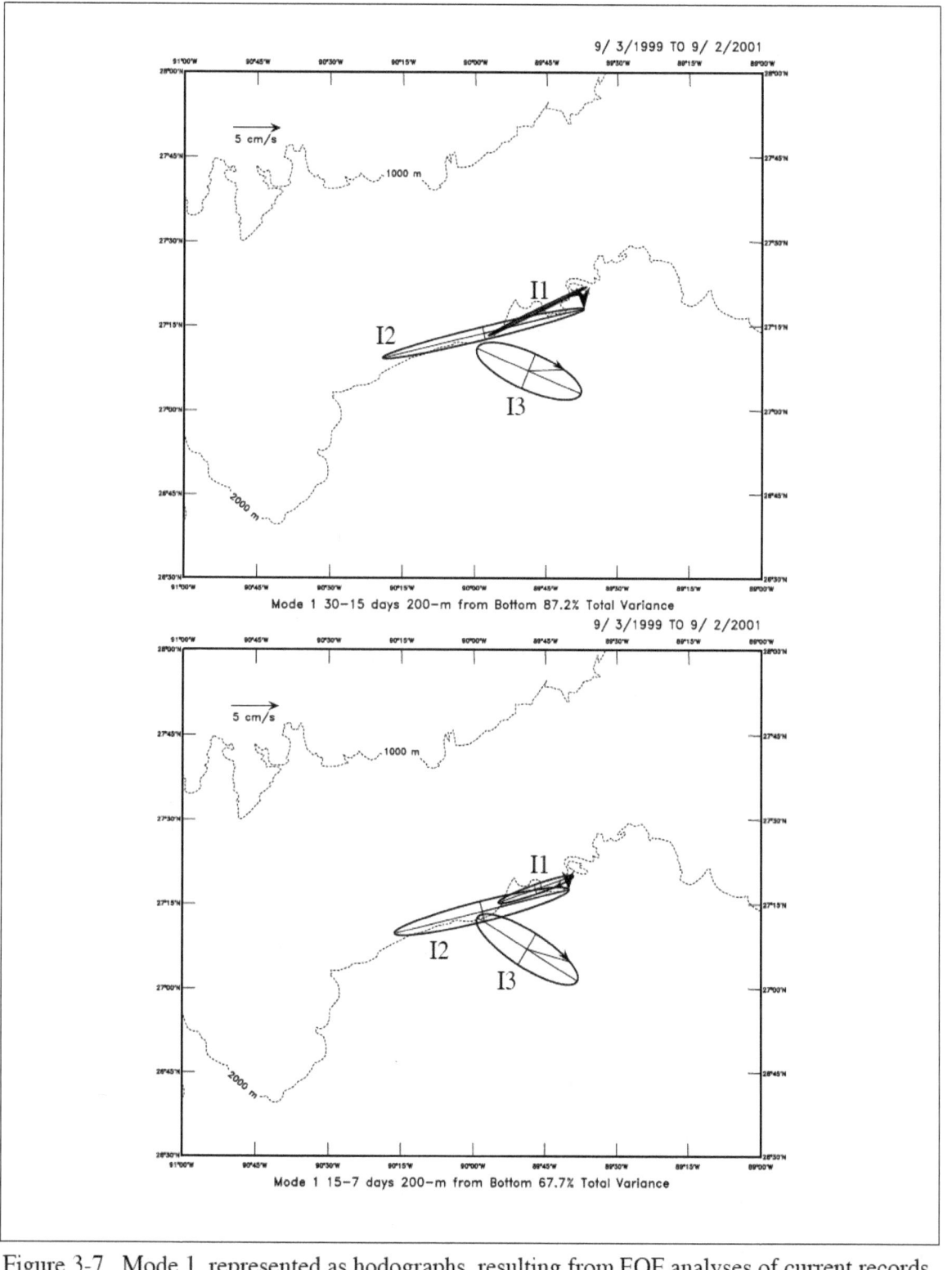

Figure 3-7. Mode 1, represented as hodographs, resulting from EOF analyses of current records 200 m from the bottom for the two-year period using frequency bands 30-15 days (upper panel), and 15-7 days (lower panel).

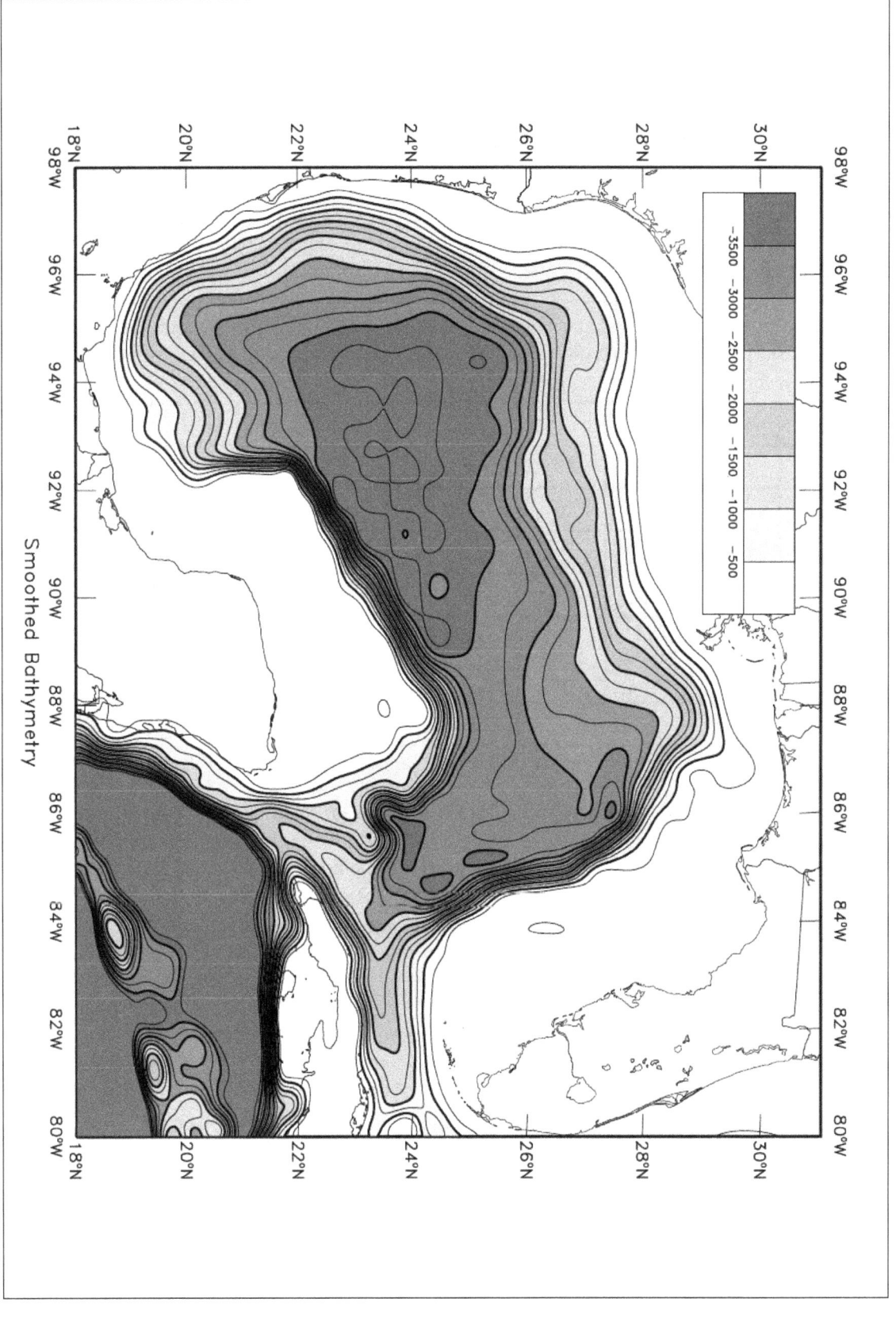

Figure 3-8. Bathymetry after applying a 50 km median filter and smoothing splines to GOTOPO 30 gridded data. Depths are in meters.

Figure 3-9. The 8-day wave in period 5 had the same wavelength as period 1. The starting point was the center of the triangle formed by the positions of I1, I2 and I3.

The backward ray traces, with negative initial upslope wavenumber components, begin east and south of the site as might be expected if the LC is involved with their generation. If a positive upslope wavenumber component is used for the backward trace then the ray paths are in shallow slope water to the north and east (Figure 3-9). Very limited evidence from moorings indicate that bottom energy is low in these regions. In particular, the DeSoto Canyon Eddy Intrusion Study (Hamilton et al. 2000) had moorings on the 1200 m isobath near the path of the 20-day wave. Energy at the near-bottom current meters was small with rms amplitudes < 3 cm/s though 20-day periods were present in the spectra. Therefore, it seems unlikely that large amplitude fluctuations observed at the site originate from these regions. Similarly, forward ray traces with negative upslope wavenumber, that continue the paths which originated in the south and east, continue into shallower water. Again, the evidence from the J1 and I4 moorings, as well as deepwater moorings, in water depths less than 2000 m, on 92°W (Hamilton, 1990), indicate that high energy at the site was not propagating directly west along the escarpment or above the escarpment. Therefore, an explanation of the decrease in energy across the escarpment is that the upslope propagating TRW's are reflected in the region of the site. The ambiguous directions,

Table 3-4. TRW Initial Conditions with Start and End Wavelengths.

Analysis Period	Initial Wave Period (days)	Initial Wavelength (km)	Initial Group Speed c_g (cm/s)	Backward		Forward	
				Start Time (days)	Wave-length (km)	End Time (days)	Wave-length (km)
1 & 5	8	76	9.4	-11.5	56	+12	86
2	12.5	50	8.4	-41	64	+34	56
3	13	62	10.4	-32	100	+29	69
4	14	70	12.0	-31	160	+27	75
5	20	87	15.9	-12	300	+37	225

relative to the bathymetry, of the principal axes of I1 and I2 have been discussed previously. If reflection occurs, and the upslope wavenumber component changes sign, the forward ray traces show paths to the south and west. The 8-day wave does not penetrate far, but the 20-day wave reaches the center of the basin in about 35 days. The lower-layer current observations made at 92°W, 25.7°N (Mooring GG in; Hamilton, 1990) showed prominent oscillations, with maximum amplitudes < 20 cm/s, with periods of 20 – 25 days. The 20-day forward ray path passes within about 50 km of this position.

Based on the analysis of periods and initial wavelengths, the rays were traced backwards and forwards from the site position with the assumption that reflection occurred. The results are shown in Figure 3-10 for all the analysis periods (see Table 3-4). The elapsed times to the start and ends of the rays, where the site position is t=0, are given in Table 3-4, along with the average wavelength found for the last two days of each forward and backward integration. For wave

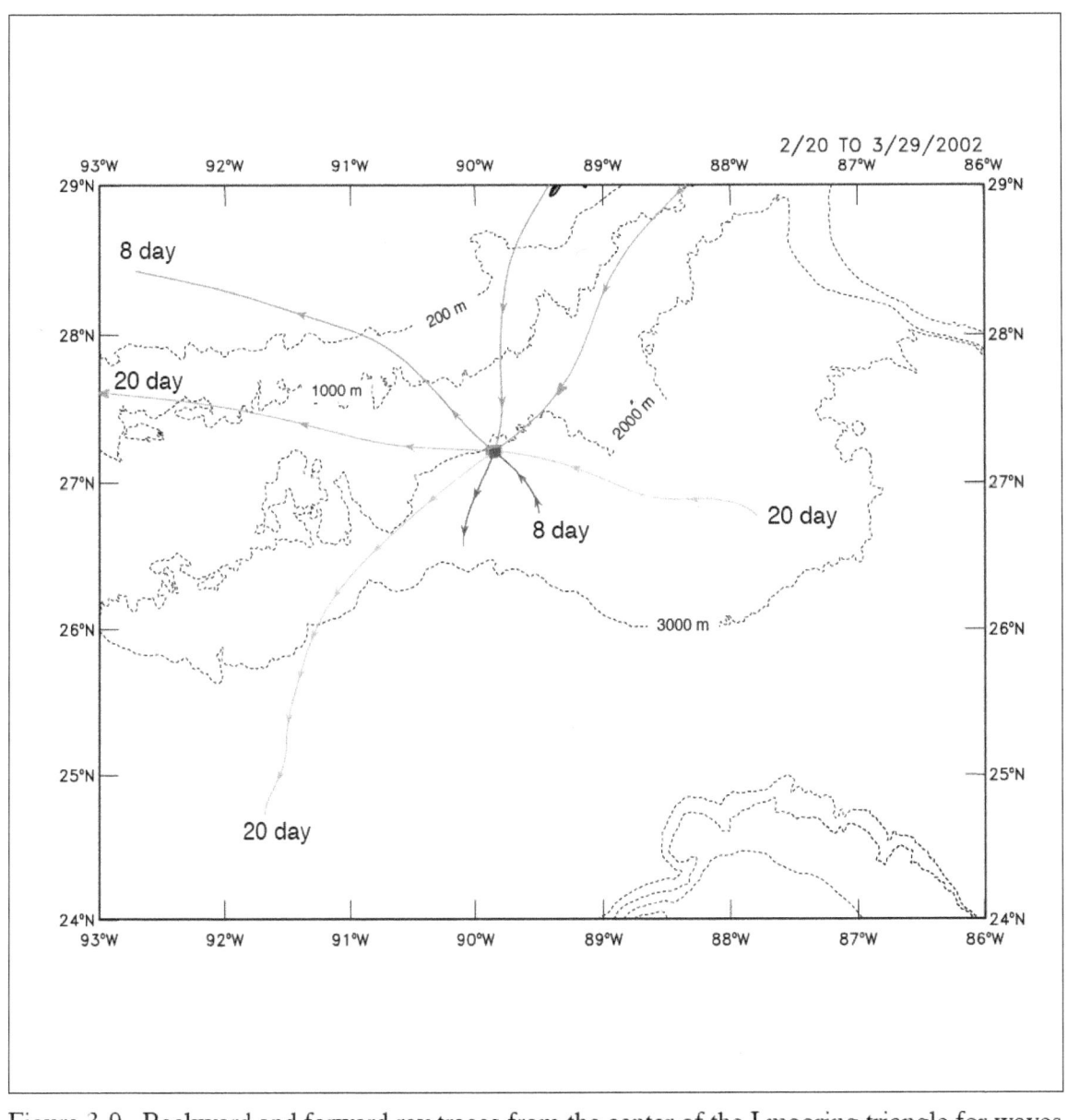

Figure 3-9. Backward and forward ray traces from the center of the I mooring triangle for waves of 8-day period and 76 km initial wavelength (blue and red), and 20-day period and 87 km wavelength (tan and green). Arrow heads are at 5-day intervals. Ray paths to the SE and NW (NE and SW) have down (up) slope directed initial phase vectors.

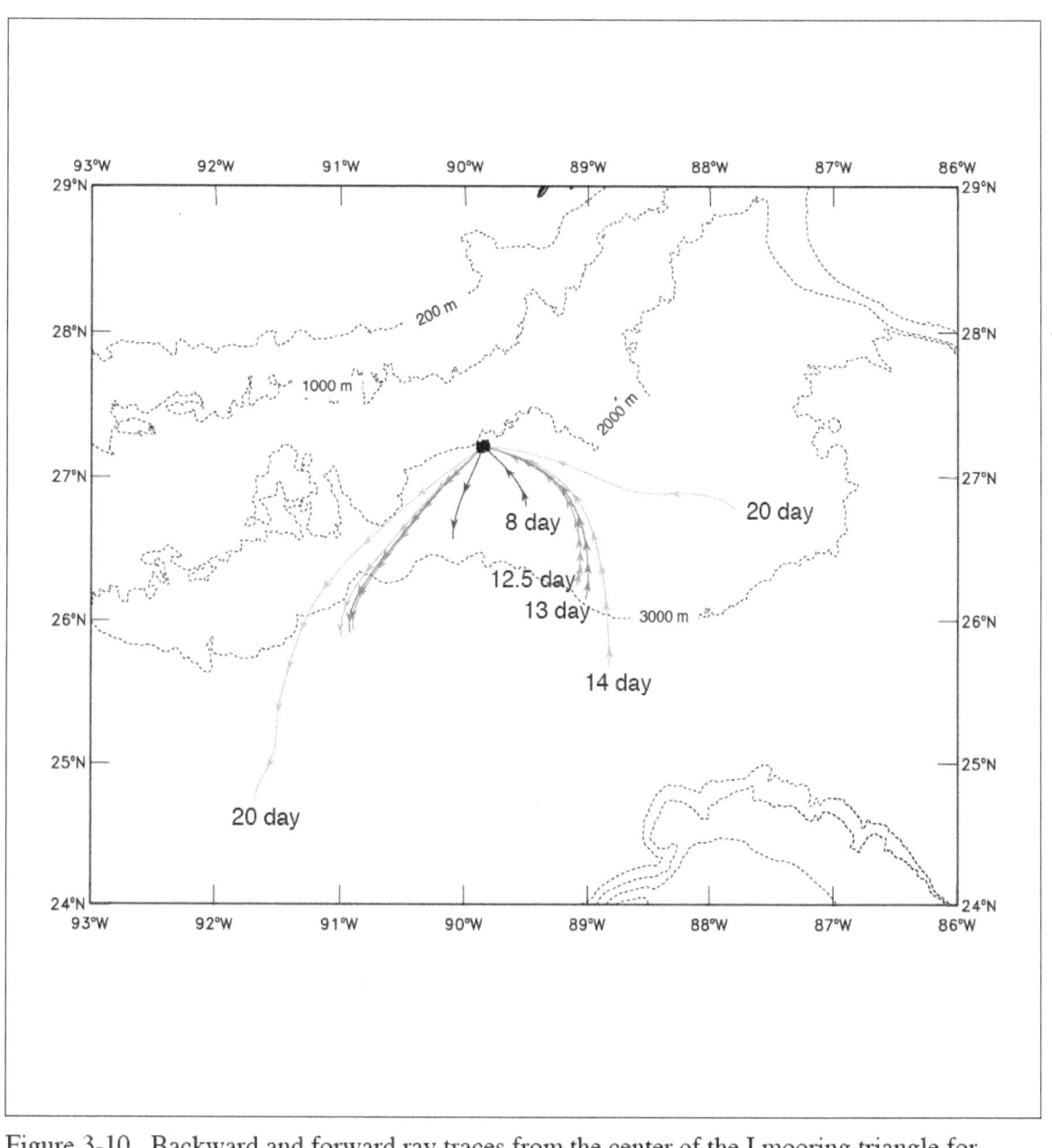

Figure 3-10. Backward and forward ray traces from the center of the I mooring triangle for waves with indicated periods. Initial wavelengths are given in Table 3-4. Arrow heads are at 5-day intervals. Ray paths to the SE (SW) have down (up) slope directed initial phase vectors.

periods less than 14 days, the generation zone appears to be on the west side of the LC and the shorter the period the more likely the generation takes place close to the site. This was noted for the fluctuations associated with peripheral cyclones that had some degree of coherence through the water column at I1 at the beginnings of periods 1, 2 and 5. Thus, this is consistent with Pickart's resonance theory of TRW generation in that rapidly northwards moving cyclones on the west side of the LC would have the right length and time scales to couple with lower layer TRWs. This is a region of explosive growth of peripheral frontal eddies as the LC flows northwards past the Campeche Bank. The ray tracing also indicates that this short period energy is confined to a region between 88.5° and 91.5°W, north of about 3000 m water depth and south of the escarpment. This agrees with the observations that energetic propagating signals with periods less than about 16 days were not observed in the deep water on the east side of the LC and west of 92°W (Hamilton, 1990). This may explain why the energy of the lower-layer currents at the site was so exceptionally large, if the TRW's are partially trapped in its vicinity.

A longer wavelength 20-day TRW is able to penetrate into the central basin as indicated by the observations. The origin of these waves is more over the Mississippi Fan and may be associated with an eddy shedding event because the wavelengths in this region are quite large (Table 3-4). However, the travel time to the site is about the same as the 8-day TRWs and this may explain why both period TRW's appearred at about the same time in period 5, as Eddy M was in the process of being shed.

In the theory of TRW motions, waves do not propagate at frequencies above $N\alpha$, where α is the bottom slope perpendicular to the isobaths. Therefore, short period waves propagating into regions of decreasing bottom slope will eventually become evanescent. This is indicated in the ray tracing when the group-velocity becomes very small and the calculation is terminated. To the author's knowledge, the behavior of TRW motions where the bottom slope decreases has not been investigated either analytically or numerically. Since linear TRW's can only propagate with shallow water on the right of the direction of propagation, reflection appears to be unlikely. Therefore, it is speculated that in this situation, wave motions must dissipate or be transformed into different types of planetary waves, perhaps changing frequencies and wavelengths by non-linear processes. Evidence from observations (Hamilton, 1990) and models (Oey and Lee, 2002) indicate that longer period (> 20 days) TRW's can reach the western Gulf, however, the paths of such waves seem to be complex with possible contributing sources from the LC and westward propagating LCE's.

The features of the TRW wave parameters and the distribution of energy by measurement interval across the site moorings suggest that TRW genesis is at multiple sites along the LC front and these change with time as the LC extends and sheds major anticyclones. Reflection of TRWs by the escarpment appears to be consistent with the observations, however, the dynamics of this process and the effects of trapping energy in a small part of the lower Gulf slope have not yet been studied either theoretically or with numerical simulations. This seems quite different from the Mid-Atlantic Bight where Gulf Stream generated 40-day period TRWs propagate large distances over the slope region (Pickart, 1995). The similarity of these observations to Hogg's (2000) measurements over the slope of the Grand Banks has been noted.

3.7   Upper Layer Circulations

The upper layer currents at I1 have been described in Section 2.3. Energetic events were dominated by Eddies J and M. Eddy J's path was further to the south than the later eddy, and mooring I1 was primarily affected by events on the periphery of its main circulation. Documentation of these events in the upper 100 m was hampered by the failure of the ADCP at 90 m after the middle of October 1999. Eddy M, on the other hand, affected the mooring between March and May 2001, during which time the mooring was measuring currents within the core of the eddy. Previous surveys of LC eddy currents have been ship-based (Cooper et al. 1990). The high-resolution temperature and current measurements on mooring I1 allow another view of the vertical and horizontal structures of part of a major LC eddy. To analyze the radial and azimuthal velocity components of Eddy M, it is necessary to identify its center path, as it moved past the mooring. The location of an eddy center is often difficult using remote sensing data. However, satellite-tracked (ARGOS) drifters were deployed in Eddy M by Horizon Marine as part of the industry program "Eddy Watch". The "Far Horizon Drifters" used in that program have a parachute-like drogue at a nominal depth of 50 m. The original data is proprietary to Horizon Marine. Use of the drifter tracks for Eddy M was purchased by the present study and two of these paths have been analyzed to provide the estimates of the locations of the center as it evolved between 89° and 91.5°W. The method uses the Glenn et al. (1990) translating ellipse kinematic model as adapted by Hamilton et al. (1999). The drifter tracks were initially smoothed and resampled at 6-hour intervals as discussed in Hamilton et al. (1999). The model uses a least-square fit of a diverging, translating ellipse to smoothed drifter paths. The equations fit to a drifter orbit are:

$$x(t) = x_0 + ut + (1 + Dt)[a\cos\theta \, \cos(-\omega t + \phi) - b\sin\theta \, \sin(-\omega t + \phi)] \qquad (5)$$

$$y(t) = y_0 + vt + (1 + Dt)[a\sin\theta \, \cos(-\omega t + \phi) + b\cos\theta \, \sin(-\omega t + \phi)] \qquad (6)$$

where

x, y	are the coordinates of the modeled drifter track;
x_0, y_0	is the t = 0 center position of the ellipse;
u, v	are the x and y components of the center translation velocity;
a, b	are the major and minor axes of the ellipse;
θ	is the inclination of the major axis to east;
ω	is the orbital frequency;
ϕ	is the t = 0 phase of the orbit;
D	is the divergence.

The orbits are fit for t ε [-T/2,T/2], where T = 2π/ω is the orbital period. Latitudes and longitudes are transformed to (x, y) coordinates using standard f – plane projections. The results of the model fits are shown in Figure 3-11 where the center paths and major and minor axes are shown for two drifters (00815 and 00850) orbiting in Eddy M. The orbital periods during this time were fairly constant at about 8 to 10 days. Some of the early orbits of 00815 were large and had longer periods, indicating that the drifter was probably outside the eddy's core. After the parameters were estimated, the distance from the center, on a given day, to the mooring position was easily calculated (Figure 3-12). The position of the major axis allows the mooring to be placed in a quadrant of the eddy. The angle, A, is defined as $\alpha - \theta$, where $\tan^{-1}\alpha = (y_m - y_0)/(x_m - x_0)$, and (x_m, y_m) is the position of the mooring (Figure 3-12). Therefore, if A is ~ 0 or $\pm 180°$, then the mooring is closest to the location of the major axis, and if A is $\sim \pm 90°$, then the mooring is closest to the position of the minor axis. The orbit solutions (5) and (6) can be used to estimate the velocity at the mooring caused by the eddy, if solid body rotation holds from the center to the mooring location. The position, B, of the drifter when it crosses the line between the mooring and the center is given by $t = t_B$, which is the solution to

$$(y_m - y_0)(x(t) - x_0) = (y(t) - y_0)(x_m - x_0) \qquad (7)$$

Using (5) and (6), the orbit is redefined to go through (x_m, y_m) for new values of a and b, subject to the constraint $a'/b' = a/b$ (Figure 3-12). The eddy velocity, V_m, at the mooring is then given by $(dx/dt, dy/dt)$ for $t = t_B$ and $(a, b) = (a', b')$. The direction of V_m can then be used to define the azimuthal velocity direction at the mooring for a given day. A comparison of the time series of V_m, and one-day averaged currents at 50 m from I1, is given in Figure 3-13. While the eddy was influencing the mooring, the observed velocities at I1 and modeled drifter-based currents have very similar characteristics.

The path of Eddy M's center (Figure 3-11) shows some interesting deviations from a more usual track to the southwest (Hamilton et al. 1999). During the later half of March, the eddy made a rapid movement towards, and then away from the slope so that the path of the center forms a loop with the eddy translating eastwards for a few days after March 28. This was the closest approach (~ 50 km) of the eddy to I1. SST imagery shows that Eddy M was attached to the Loop Current through March and early April (Figure 3-14). The March 23 image shows a roughly circular eddy (see also the similar major and minor axis lengths in Figure 3-11). Soon after this, the eddy developed a large westward extrusion over the northern slope, apparently formed by a large cyclone that developed and propagated northwestward along the west side of the LC and Eddy M. The large cyclone is seen in the April 5 image (Figure 3-14), and it is likely that the interaction between the anticyclonic Eddy M and the cyclone caused the northward loop of the eddy center in late March. The warm westward extension, or large filament, eventually detached from M, in late April, as the cyclone continued to move up onto the slope. No drifters were entrained in this filament, indicating that it may not have been an active circulation feature (i.e. a separate anticyclone).

In April, the Eddy M translated due westward towards the slope, presumably because of the influence of the cyclone to its west. At the beginning of May, as the center approached the 2000 m isobath, the eddy stalled and then moved rapidly southward, away from the slope. It also became more elliptical with the major axis directed northwest to southeast. This apparent "bounce off the slope" could be a result of the shoaling depths of the slope. (In our experience, eddy centers never cross the 2000 m isobath on the eastern and central Gulf slope – see Hamilton et al. 1999; 2002). However, the path of the eddy center was similar, but more extreme, to that of Eddy Y, in November 1994, caused by interaction with a lower slope cyclone on its northwestern side (Hamilton et al. 1999; 2002). The cyclone in Figure 3-14 apparently moved onto the slope in late April and early May, and may have caused the interaction that moved Eddy M away from the slope. Available evidence (Hamilton 1992; Hamilton et al. 2002), indicates that once a large cyclone has moved onto the lower slope, it usually becomes fairly stationary

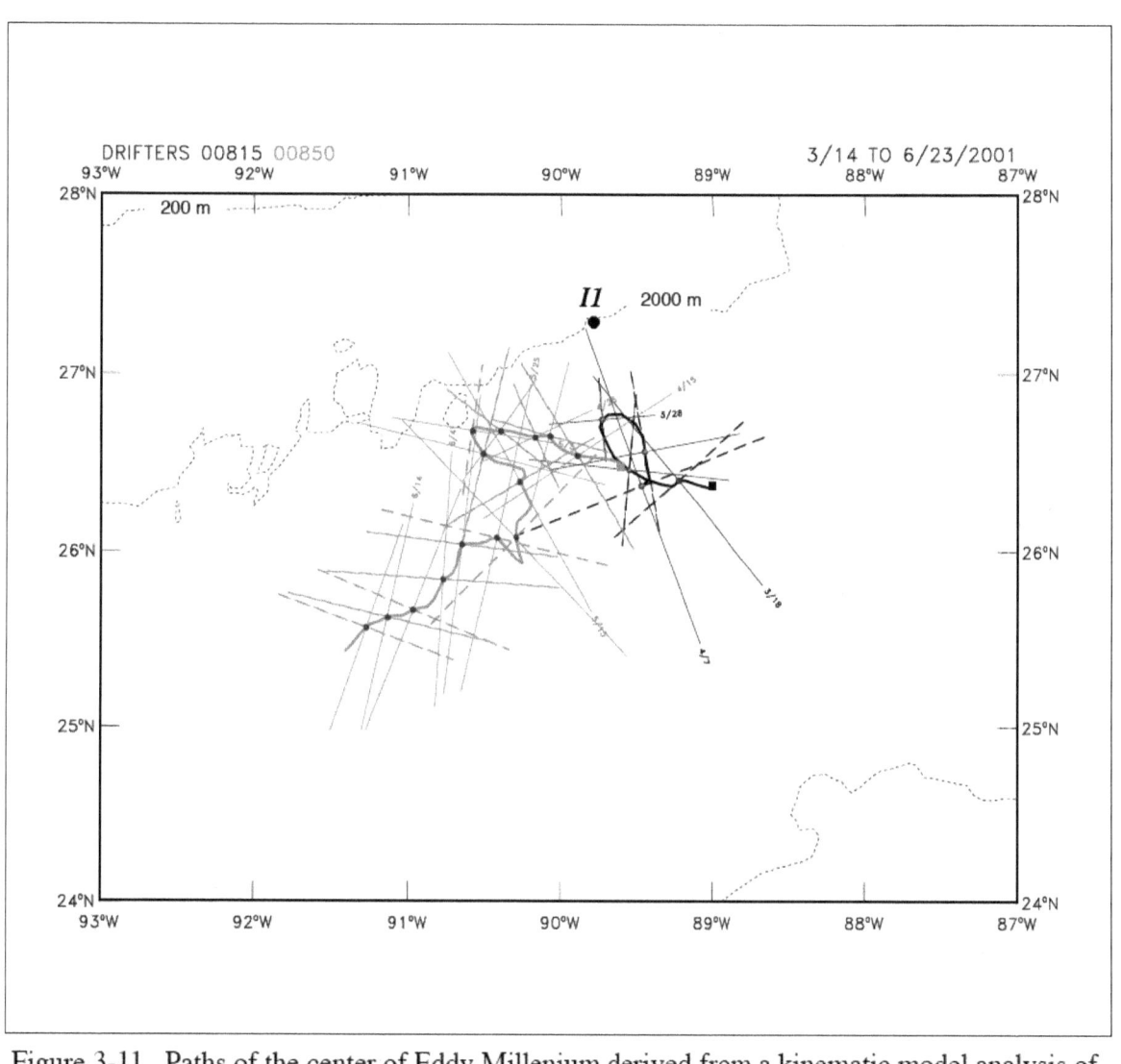

Figure 3-11. Paths of the center of Eddy Millenium derived from a kinematic model analysis of smoothed drifter tracks (heavy lines). Solid squares mark the start of each path. The major and minor (dashed) axes from the model are shown every 5 days. Dates (month/day) are given every 10 days.

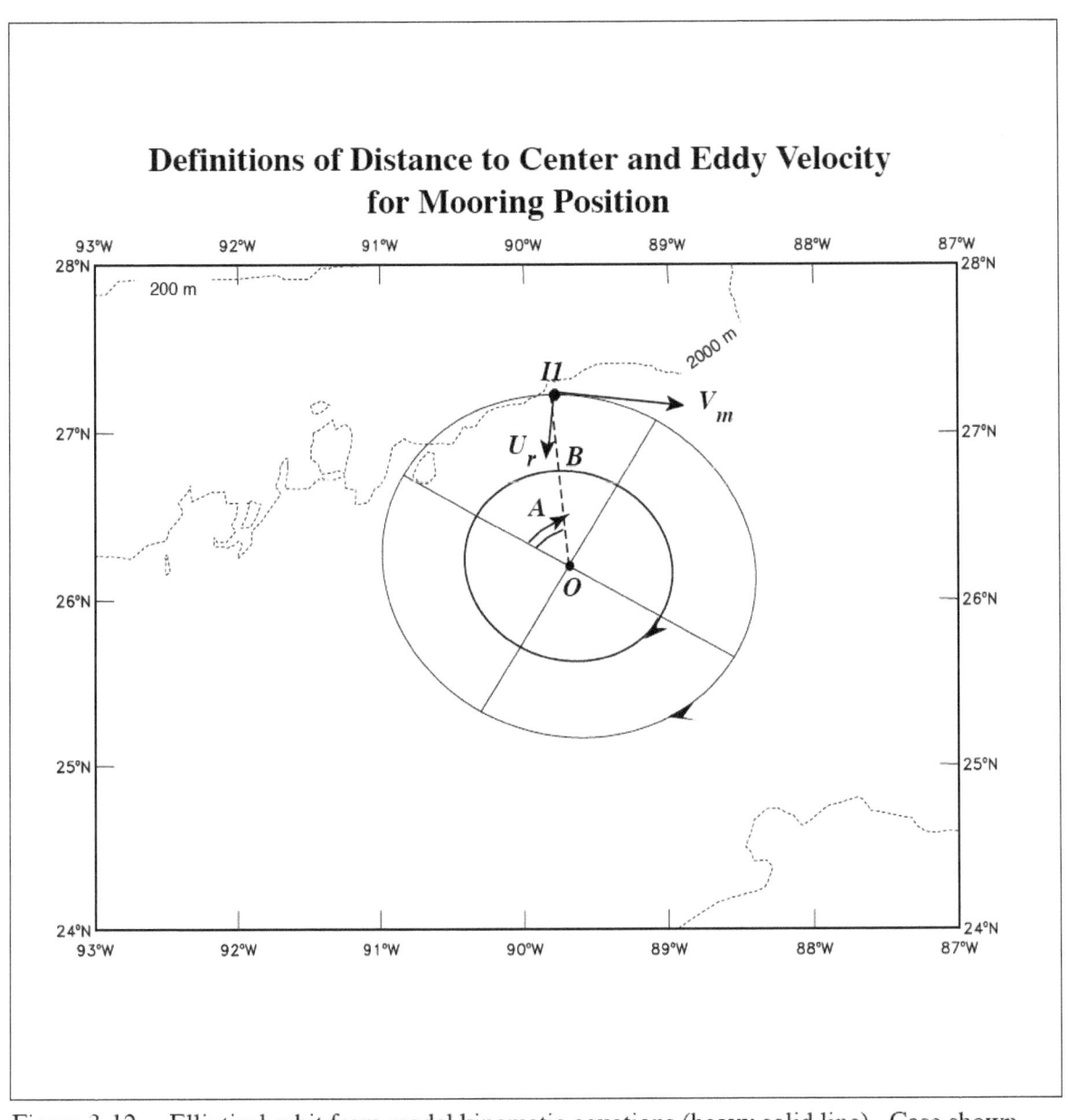

Figure 3-12. Elliptical orbit from model kinematic equations (heavy solid line). Case shown with no translation or divergence. Distance to the eddy center = *I1-O;* angle between *I1-O* and major axis = *A*. Fitted ellipse expanded to go through the site shown as thin line, which also defines the eddy velocity, V_m, assuming solid body rotation within the trajectory.

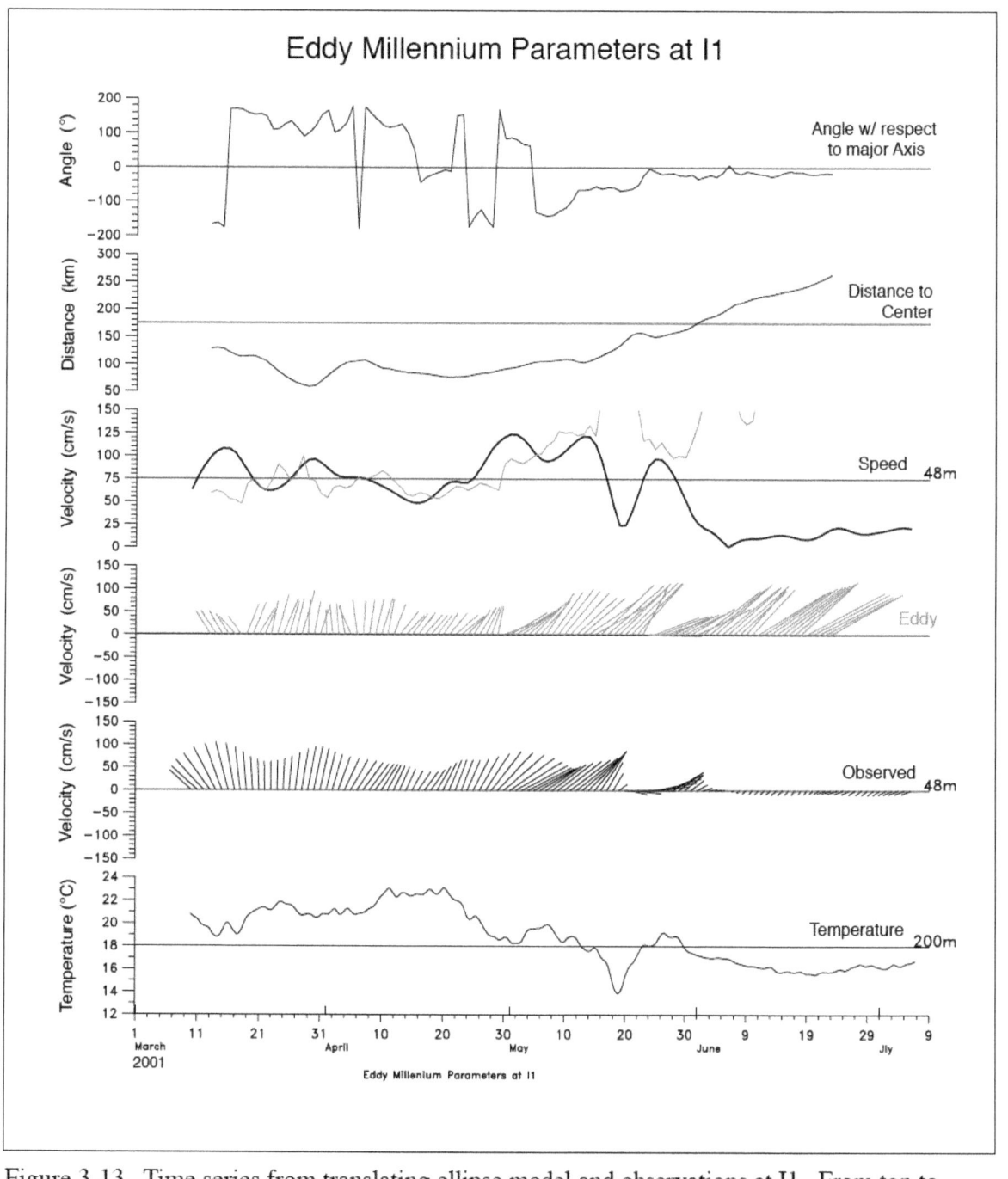

Figure 3-13. Time series from translating ellipse model and observations at I1. From top to bottom, the panels are: Angle of line to center with respect to major axis, distance from I1 to the center, current speed from one-day averaged observations at 50 m (black) and eddy model (red), eddy model current vectors at I1 (red), observed current vectors at I1, and temperature at 200 m at I1.

and would block further westward movement of a LC anticyclone to its east. Unfortunately, SST imagery was obscured by extensive cloud cover at this time, so it has not been possible to confirm directly the existence of a large lower slope cyclone around 92° to 93°W. Between May 15 and 25, the observed velocities and temperatures at I1 decrease, and the mooring was not under the direct influence of the eddy (Figures 3-12 and 3-13). Eddy M currents returned for a short period after May 25, even though the eddy was further away. The elliptical shape of the eddy and the rotation of the major axis from northwest to northeast, after the southward displacement, was the cause of this. In June, Eddy M again became more circular and had a southwestward path, approximately parallel to, and ~100 km south of, the 2000 m isobath. This is a fairly typical path for central Gulf LC eddies (see path of Eddy Y in Hamilton et al. 1999).

The azimuthal and radial velocity profiles were calculated using daily averaged 40-HLP records where the azimuthal direction is defined by the kinematic model fits to the smoothed buoy tracks as discussed above. The radial direction is defined as orthogonal to V_m (Figure 3-12) and has the opposite sign to conventional definitions of radial velocities for circular eddies (e.g. Kunze 1986). The results are given at seven-day intervals for the period March 13 (Julian Day 72) to June 5 (day 156), 2001, in Figure 3-15. The directions (relative to North), of the azimuthal components, are given by the arrows, and the distance of the mooring, from the estimated eddy center position, is given by the color scale. The velocities include the translation of the eddy. In general, the closer to the center, the more uniform with depth are the azimuthal profiles, but there are differences in profiles that fall into the same "distance from the center bins". For example, compare the azimuthal profiles for days 93, 100 and 121 (April 3, 10, and May 1). The first two dates are when the eddy was still attached to the LC, and the eddy center was looping to the north (Figure 3-11), and the latter was after the eddy had detached and was approaching the slope. Prior to detachment, two of the azimuthal profiles had maximum currents at 100 to 150 m below the surface (days 79 and 86; March 20 and 27). This is associated with a reversal of the radial velocities (most clearly seen for day 86), from divergent near the surface to convergent, in the region of the maximum, and divergent below. After day 107 (April 17), when the mooring was in the trailing quadrants of the eddy, these features in the profiles were not present. It is not known whether the increased structure in the velocity profiles in the first part of the record, compared to the later, is because the mooring was in the leading part of the eddy, or because the eddy was still attached to the LC.

The azimuthal vertical shears are expected to be related closely to the eddy temperature field through the cyclogeostrophic momentum balance (Kunze 1986). Figure 3-16 shows the vertical temperature profiles and their corresponding azimuthal velocity profiles. Thus, the warmest water at I1, on day 107 (April 17), when the 12°C isotherm reached its deepest depth, corresponds to relatively depth independent currents. The sequence of plots for days 107 to 135, show increasing shears and shoaling isotherms as would be expected for a station moving from close to the center to edges of the eddy. On day 135 (May 15), the observed 50-m current was less than the solid-body rotation current, which indicates that the mooring was in the outer cyclonic shear zone of the eddy's circulation (Figure 3-13). Of this sequence of 5 profiles, the one occurring on day 128 (May 8) is more characteristic of a position closer to the center than the profiles on either side. The isotherms, however, had only slightly deepened from day 121. May 8 was during the interval when the eddy moved rapidly to the southeast and elongated. Therefore, the interaction with the slope cyclone appears to have increased the radius of the region of solid body rotation and the mooring appears to have been relatively nearer the center. Some of the velocity in the upper 600 m for this profile was caused by the southeastward translation as can be seen by the positive radial component in Figure 3-15. This analysis indicates that the motion of the eddy and its interactions with surrounding circulation features could change swirl and radial velocity fields from that expected by a fixed –size translating elliptical bowl shaped circulations. The last part of the eddy velocity record at I1 can be used to estimate the width of the cyclonic shear zone. On May 25 (day 145), eddy and observed speeds were similar (Figure 3-13). By June 5, the observed speeds had dropped to zero as the eddy moved away from the site at a fairly constant speed. During this interval, the orientations of the ellipse major axis were fairly constant and directed towards I1. This indicates that the length of the semi-major axis or the distance from the center to the maximum surface velocity was ~ 150 km. Using the drifter calculated a/b for May 25, results in the estimate for the semi-minor axis of ~ 100 km. The width of the cyclonic shear zone, where the swirl velocities decrease from a maximum to zero, is about 50 km. Thus, a rough estimate of the cylonic shear zone width was ~1/3 the eddy radius to the maximum swirl velocity. This would indicate that the positive vorticity anomaly associated with the outer edges of the eddy is about three times the negative vorticity anomaly associated with the eddy core. Using a rotation period of 9 days, the relative vorticity of the eddy is ~ -0.13f. Therefore, the high positive vorticity anomaly associated with the cyclonic shear zone implies instabilities and non-linear dynamics.

The profiles can also be used to estimate the changes in horizontal velocity shear within the eddy with depth. The azimuthal velocities were corrected for the translation of the eddy by subtracting the center velocity vector for each day. These swirl velocities were then plotted as a function of distance from the eddy center for five selected depths from the daily profiles for the March 13 to June 5, period. The May 19 to 21 period, when the edge of the eddy briefly moved away from the mooring (Figure 3-13), was excluded. The results are given in Figure 3-17. There is scatter because of the evolving velocity fields and the elliptical shape, which results in higher velocities closer to the center when the minor axis is directed towards I1 and vice-versa. The lines on the plots are subjective attempts to define the anticyclonic and cyclonic shear zones, interior and exterior to the velocity maximum at each depth, respectively. Both the cyclonic and anticyclonic shears decrease with depth with the former showing the larger relative decrease. This is because the interior of the eddy is closer to solid body rotation, particularly in the upper 100 m. Since the maximum velocity occurs closer to the center with increasing depth, and the eddy velocities fall to zero at about the same distance (~ 200 km) from the center, the cyclonic shears become weaker with depth. Thus, the positive relative vorticity region has strong depth gradients, where as the eddy interior has a more uniform negative vorticities. The radial fields of swirl velocities suggested by Figure 3-17 are more complex than used by most eddy models that assume depth independence and/or isolation from surrounding waters.

3.8 Inertial Currents

High frequency currents in deep-water regions of the northern Gulf are dominated by inertial oscillations. These are clockwise rotating currents (viewed from above) with periods near but

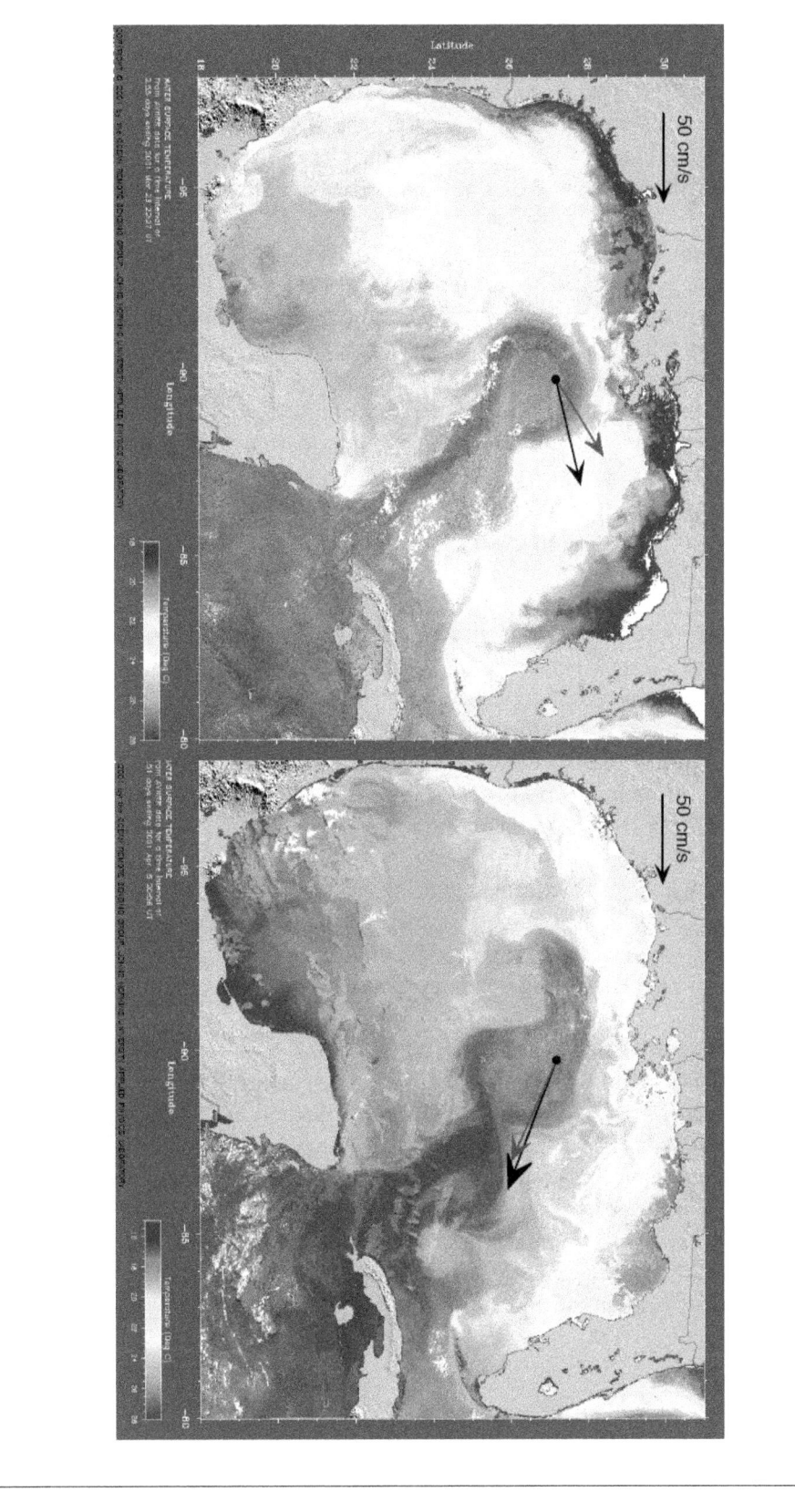

Figure 3-14. Composite AVHRR Images for March 23 (left panel) and April 5 (right panel), 2001 (Courtesy John Hopkins University Applied Physics Laboratory). One day mean 40-HLP velocities from I1, centered on these times, are overlaid for 50 and 250 m depth (black and purple arrows, respectively).

shorter than $2\pi/f_e$, where f_e, the effective Coriolis parameter given by (Mooers, 1975), is defined as:

$$f_e^2 = f (f + \zeta)$$

where ζ is the relative vorticity of the background current field. At mooring I1, the inertial period, $2\pi/f$, is 26.2 hours (frequency 0.92 cpd). At periods longer than $2\pi/f_e$, inertial waves cannot propagate. The background vorticity field of an anticyclone is negative in the center surrounded by a positive annulus where the anticyclone is not in solid body rotation. Inertial energy can be trapped in the center of the eddy by this type of vorticity field and this leads to enhanced inertial velocities (Kunze, 1985; 1986). Inertial-internal waves propagate horizontally and vertically though vertical group velocities are small (Lighthill, 1978). Thus, at positions below the surface, inertial wave packets can exhibit slightly different frequencies and propagation characteristics, since they may have propagated from different source regions.

The sources of inertial oscillations are generally rapid changes in atmospheric forcing. Thus, hurricanes over deep water usually generate strong inertial wakes. Examples in the Gulf of Mexico include Hurricanes Allen (Brooks, 1983), Frederic (Shay and Elsberry, 1987), Georges and Earl (Hamilton et al. 2000). Surface inertial current magnitudes of ~ 100 cm/s are not uncommon during the passage of major hurricanes and the oscillations can persist several days or even weeks after the hurricane has left the area. Other sources of inertial currents are winter storms. Over the DeSoto Canyon slope region to the east of the delta, Hamilton et al. (2000) found persistent inertial oscillations in the upper water column throughout the year. The ubiquitous nature of these upper-layer inertial currents, particularly in summer, was partly ascribed to trapping by the vorticity of the lower slope eddies and the eastward flowing slope jet. This was in contrast to the Louisiana-Texas shelf-break region to the west of the delta where Chen et al. (1996) found that near inertial energy could be related to storms and decayed rapidly seaward of the shelf-break.

The records at I1 contain events for two winters and two LC eddies. No major hurricanes or tropical storms passed near the site during the two-year deployment period. A short section of the 3-HLP current records from I1 are shown in Figure 3-18. The nearly daily period fluctuations were present at all depths above about 800 m. Amplitudes varied with time and different depth levels varied in intensity. Around the depth of the main thermocline, at 250 m, the fluctuations were relatively more energetic and sustained in time, suggesting that trapping may have been occurring. Generally, however, amplitudes decayed with depth as would be expected for surface forced oscillations. The v-components lead the u-components by about 90° which indicates clockwise rotation of the current vectors. At this site inertial current oscillations did not penetrate deeper than about 1200 m.

To determine how inertial current magnitudes vary over the two-year duration of the mooring deployments, complex demodulation (Priestley, 1981) was performed for all current records in the upper layer using a period of 26 hours. A running 52-hour mean was subtracted from the records and the results filtered with a 4-Day Low Pass Lanzcos kernel. The amplitudes at selected depths are given in Figure 3-19 where the speeds of the 40-HLP winds from the C-MAN meteorological station (see Figure 1-1) at the southwestern tip of the Mississippi delta (BURL1)

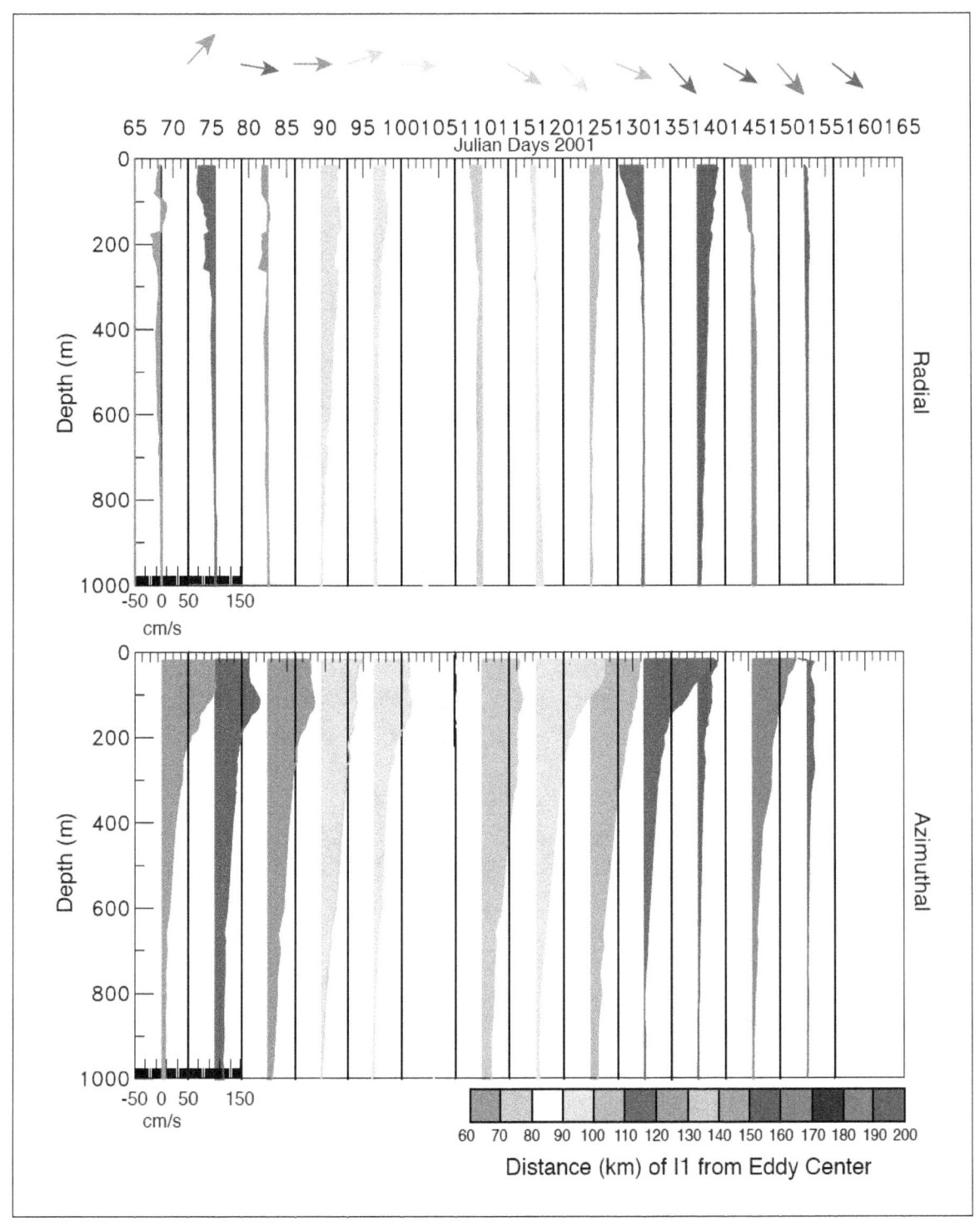

Figure 3-15. Radial (U_r-upper panel) and azimuthal (V_m-lower panel) components of daily averaged velocity profiles, at I1, for eddy M on the given Julian days, 2001. The profiles are color coded according to distance from the eddy center. The vectors, above the plots, show the direction of the azimuthal component as defined in Figure 3-12.

61

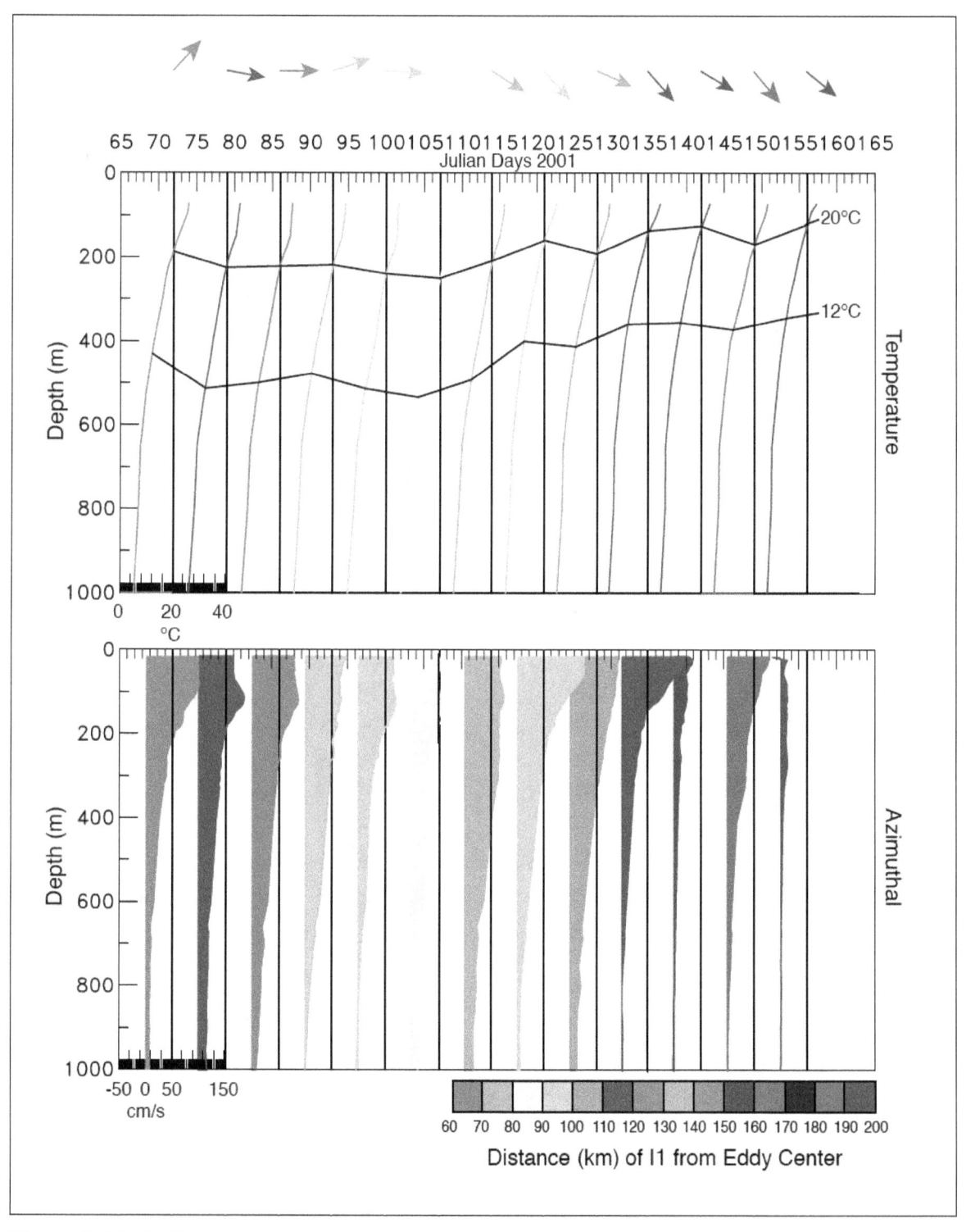

Figure 3-16. Daily averaged temperature (upper panel) and azimuthal (V_m-lower panel) velocity component profiles, at I1, for eddy M on the given Julian days, 2001. The profiles are color coded according to distance from the eddy center. The vectors, above the plots, show the direction of the azimuthal component as defined in Figure 3-12.

62

are also displayed. Intervals with high currents caused by Eddies J and M and their associated cyclones (see Figure 2-2) are also indicated. During the passage of Eddy J, the 90-m level ADCP did not produce any data after October 1999, so it is unclear whether the upper layer had enhanced inertial activity. However, at 126 m depth during December and January, energy levels were elevated. At this time, the 126 m level was above the main thermocline (Figure 2-4) and therefore, this may be an indication of trapping within the ring. Below the thermocline, amplitudes (< 5 cm/s) were quite small except for occasional bursts (e.g. at 428 m at the end of September and the beginning of November). Between March and October 2000, when surface-layer eddy currents were weak, and wind speeds relatively low, inertial amplitudes were also small at all depths. In October, November and December 2001, when eddy currents were still weak, inertial amplitudes increased in the upper 100 m of the water column, somewhat corresponding to the increased in storm activity in the fall and early winter. In January and February 2001, inertial amplitudes increase dramatically in the near surface, even though wind events were no stronger than in the fall and a little less frequent. This interval was characterized by vigorous currents associated with cyclones that preceded Eddy M, suggesting that eddy-eddy interactions may have been generating these inertial currents. As Eddy M moved over the site, inertial amplitudes decreased in the near surface but increased at deeper levels corresponding to the increasing depth of the thermocline (see the 16°C isotherm in Figure 2-4b). This again suggests that the inertial energy generated in January and February propagated downward into the approaching warm eddy and appears to have been trapped in the negative vorticity region above the thermocline. In July and August 2001, after Eddy M had moved into the western Gulf, there was again strong currents caused by cyclones associated with the LC (Figure 2-3j and k), and again there was an increase in inertial amplitudes in the near surface, even though winds were weak, as is typical of the summer period.

Based on the above discussion, more detailed analysis of inertial motions was carried out for three two-month interals corresponding to parts of the records with large amplitude oscillations in the surface layer. These are 1) October 27 to December 25, 2000, when low-frequency currents were quiescent; 2) January 1 to March 1, 2001, when cyclones were present; and 3) March 1 to April 29, 2001, when Eddy M was over the site (Figure 3-19). These periods had good depth coverage from 20 m to 1000 m, except for a gap between 410 and 600 m. Spectra from four representative depths in the upper 400 m, for the three intervals, are given in Figure 3-20. The spectra are for velocities that have been decomposed into anticlockwise (+) and clockwise (-) rotating components (Gonella, 1971). Only the frequency band around the inertial period, $f = 0.917$ cpd, is shown and for all the spectra the clockwise rotating component dominated over the anticlockwise, which is characteristic of inertial currents in the upper layers of the ocean. In the first interval, the peaks of the spectra are at frequencies that are 5 to 10% greater than f. Amplitudes decreased with depth and the energy was spread over a broad range of frequencies that is a consequence of spectral analysis of highly intermittent signals. In the second interval, clockwise amplitudes increased at the deeper levels and the spectral peaks were more centered about f. The near surface level (20 m) had a peak at a frequency at about 5% less than f. This could indicate that this signal was not propagating (i.e., evanescent), or was being generated in a region that had negative (anticyclonic) relative vorticity, and was therefore, probably trapped in the surface layer. In Eddy M, the relative vorticity of the core was negative and f_e decreased. Thus, in interval three, the spectral peaks, except at 20 m, were at frequencies that are more than 10% less than f, and the energy levels at the three deeper depths had increased

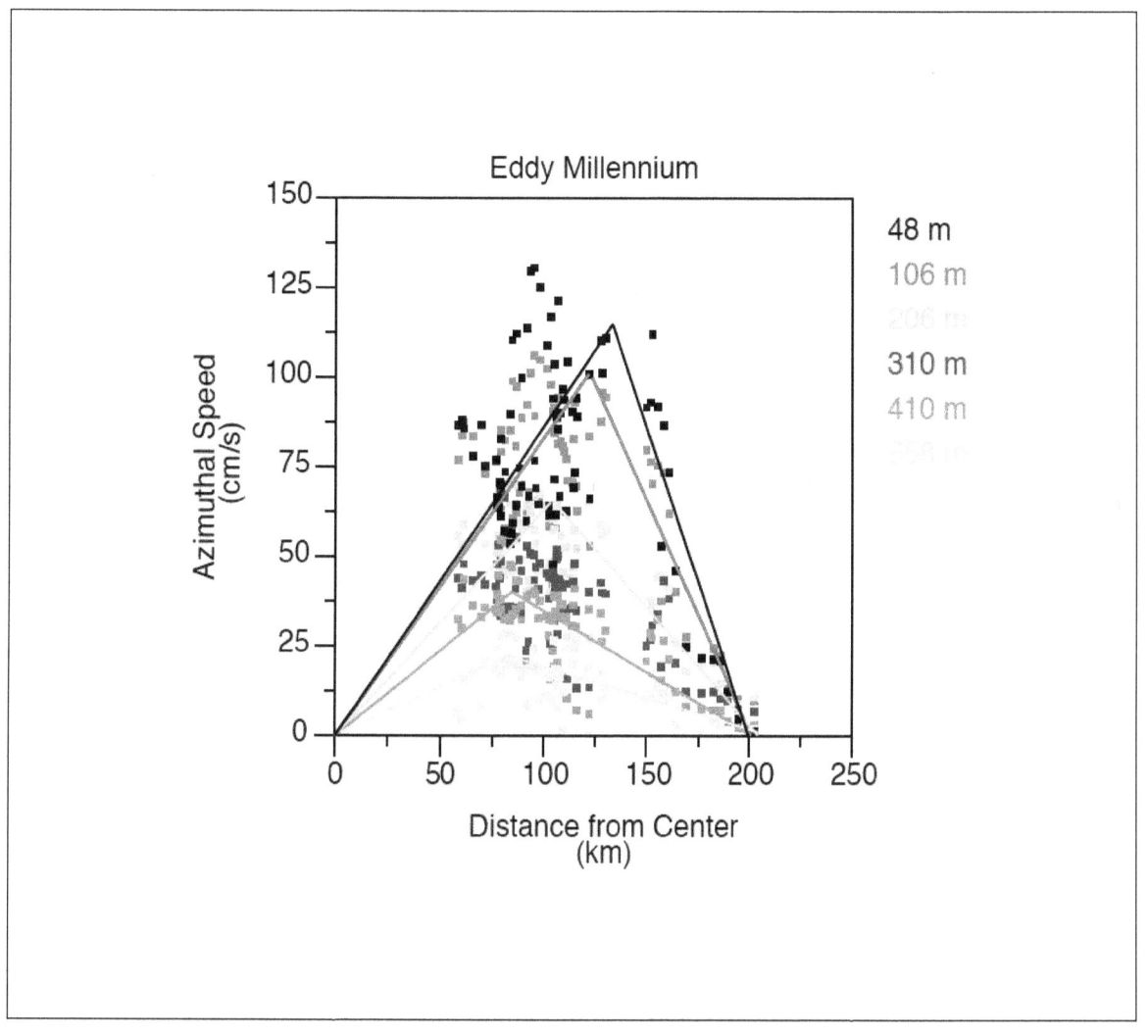

Figure 3-17. Azimuthal velocities (adjusted for effects of eddy translation) as a function of distance from the center of the eddy for the period March 13 to June 5 (excluding May 19 -21). Depths are indicated by the color code, and estimated mean shears on the cyclonic and anticyclonic sides of the maximum swirl velocity are given by the straight lines.

over interval two. The deepest level (410 m) has the highest energy levels, indicating that trapping may have been occurring at the base of the upper layer that had the anticyclonic rotation of the eddy (Kunze, 1986).

Further investigation of the depth distribution of energy in the inertial band was carried out for the three intervals by using frequency domain EOF analysis. The frequency bands were centered about the dominant spectral peaks for each interval and in all cases at least two modes were significant. Analyses were done for all depths above 1000 m and it was found that below about 400 m, amplitudes were small. Therefore, the analysis was repeated for all records above 400 m and the mode amplitudes and phases for the U and V-components are given in Figures 3-21 and 3-22. In all cases where the mode amplitudes were significant, the V-component leads the U-component by approximately 90°, and component amplitudes had similar magnitudes. This is characteristic of all clockwise (anticyclonic) rotary motions. Phases also generally increased with depth so that deeper fluctuations led those at higher levels. Upward phase propagation for internal waves indicates that energy propagation (vertical group velocity) is downwards, suggesting surface forcing. The slope of the phase lines is an indication of the vertical wavelength of the coherent motions represented by the modes (i.e. the phase changes by 360° over a vertical wavelength).

In interval one, when eddy activity was weak, mode 1 was surface intensified above 100 m with almost constant phase (Figure 3-21). This indicates slab-like motions in the upper 100 m, with no downwards flux of energy, and suggests that a well-mixed surface layer extended down to about 80 m, with these fluctuations being directly forced by local winter storms. Below the surface layer, both modes 1 and 2 had subsurface maxima at about 200 m depth. Because modes were not correlated, this suggests that the inertial waves represented by these modes had different origins, with mode 1 energy being propagated down from the local surface layer, and mode 2 perhaps from more remote regions. The depth of the 15°C isotherm (see Figure 2-4b), which is characteristic of the main thermocline, was at about 200 m at this time. Both modes had similar characteristic wavelengths of 400 to 500 m, below the surface layer.

In the next interval (Figure 3-21), the upper layers were dominated by cyclones prior to the arrival of Eddy M. Despite this positive vorticity, the spectral peaks shifted to lower frequencies when compared with the previous interval (Figure 3-20). This suggests that the inertial waves were being trapped in the outer parts of the cyclones where there was an annulus of negative vorticity surrounding the positive cores. Mode 1 was again surface intensified but the fluctuations were no longer slab-like. Depth of penetration was shallower at about 50 to 60 m, which is consistent with the uplift of the isotherms by the cyclones (Figure 2-4b). Mode 2 had a subsurface maximum at about 150 m, with implied vertical wavelengths of about 400 m. When Eddy M arrived, interval 3 amplitudes and phases (Figure 3-22) changed in character. Mode 1 was no longer surface intensified, rather showed almost constant amplitudes below 100 m and above 450 m. The vertical wavelengths were again large ($\sim$ 500 m) and coupled with the shift of the spectral peaks to frequencies less than f (Figure 3-20). This suggests trapping above the thermocline in the core of the eddy. In this interval, three modes were significant. However, modes 2 and 3 had relatively constant amplitudes in the upper 400 m and the main difference between them was vertical wavelengths of about 200 and 400 m, respectively. The significance of these latter modes is not clear, and they may just represent background inertial energy

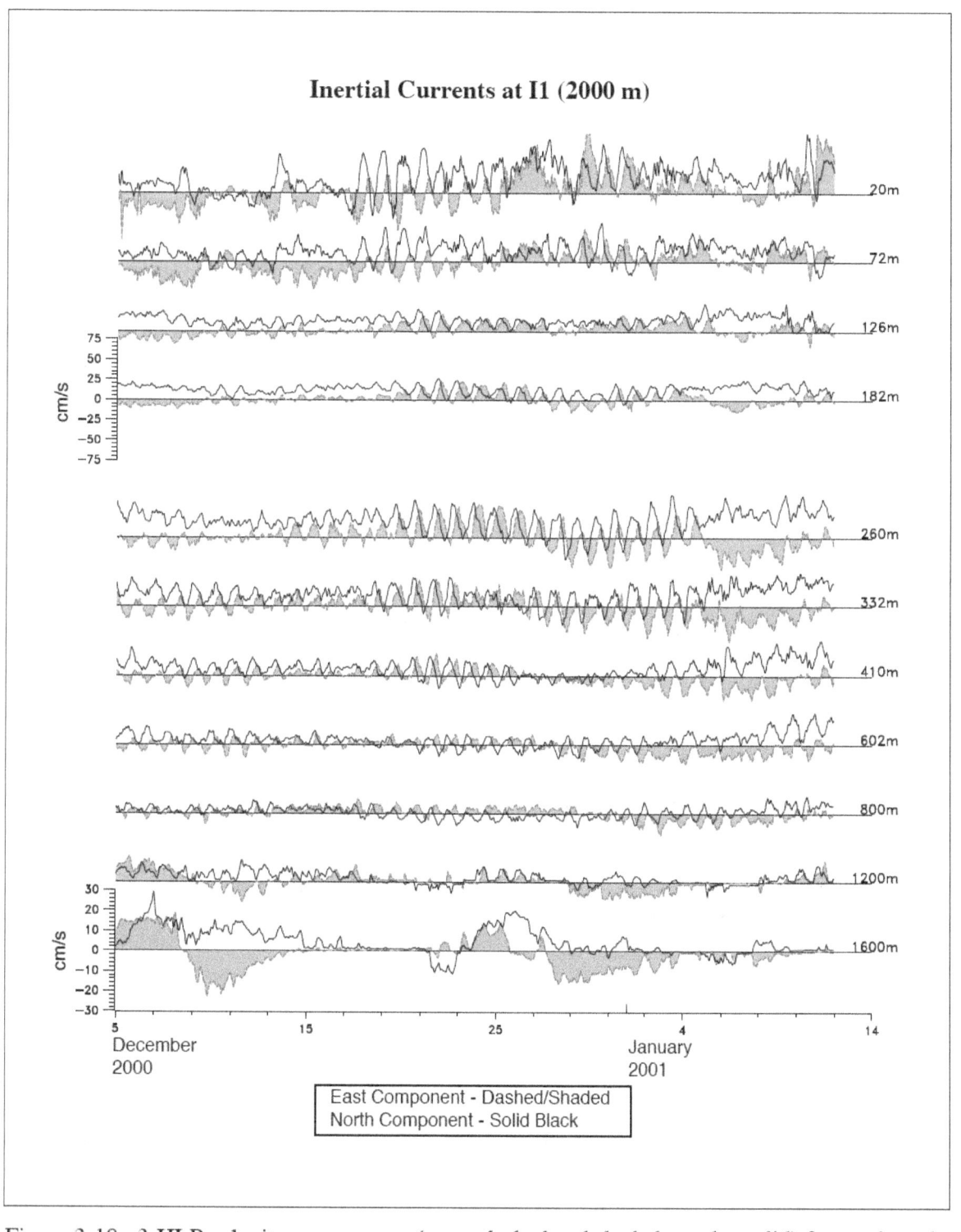

Figure 3-18. 3-HLP velocity components (east - dashed and shaded, north - solid) from selected depths of mooring I1 for the indicated period.

resulting from events earlier in this ring's history. The mode 1 results are consistent with Kunze's (1986) analysis of the trapping of inertial oscillations in a Gulf Stream warm-core ring. They also suggest that instability processes on the edge of a large anticyclone (i.e. the presence of peripheral cyclones), may have been a source of inertial energy. The high surface energies of interval 2, exceeded, for several events, the supposed wind forced response of interval 1 (Figure 3-19). The temperature profiles in the upper ocean were similar for both intervals and the winds were generally weaker in interval 2 than earlier. The strong surface-layer fluctuations then propagate horizontally and vertically into the approaching anticyclone, which showed decreasing inertial amplitudes in the surface layer and accumulation of energy at depths above the mainthermocline. This speculation cannot be proved because information on the horizontal propagation of inertial packets is lacking.

The trapping of inertial oscillations at the base of the thermocline, in rings, has been observed in the Mid-Atlantic (Kunze, 1986), and is suggested by these measurements in Eddy M. Concentration of inertial energy at depth could result in subsurface inertial jets that could be a hazard to oil industry operations. However, this type of phenomena seems most likely to occur within LCE's, and therefore the background low-frequency surface currents are likely to be energetic. This is somewhat different than reported occurrences of subsurface jet-like currents when surface currents are quiescent (DiMarco, personal communication) and LCE's were not present.

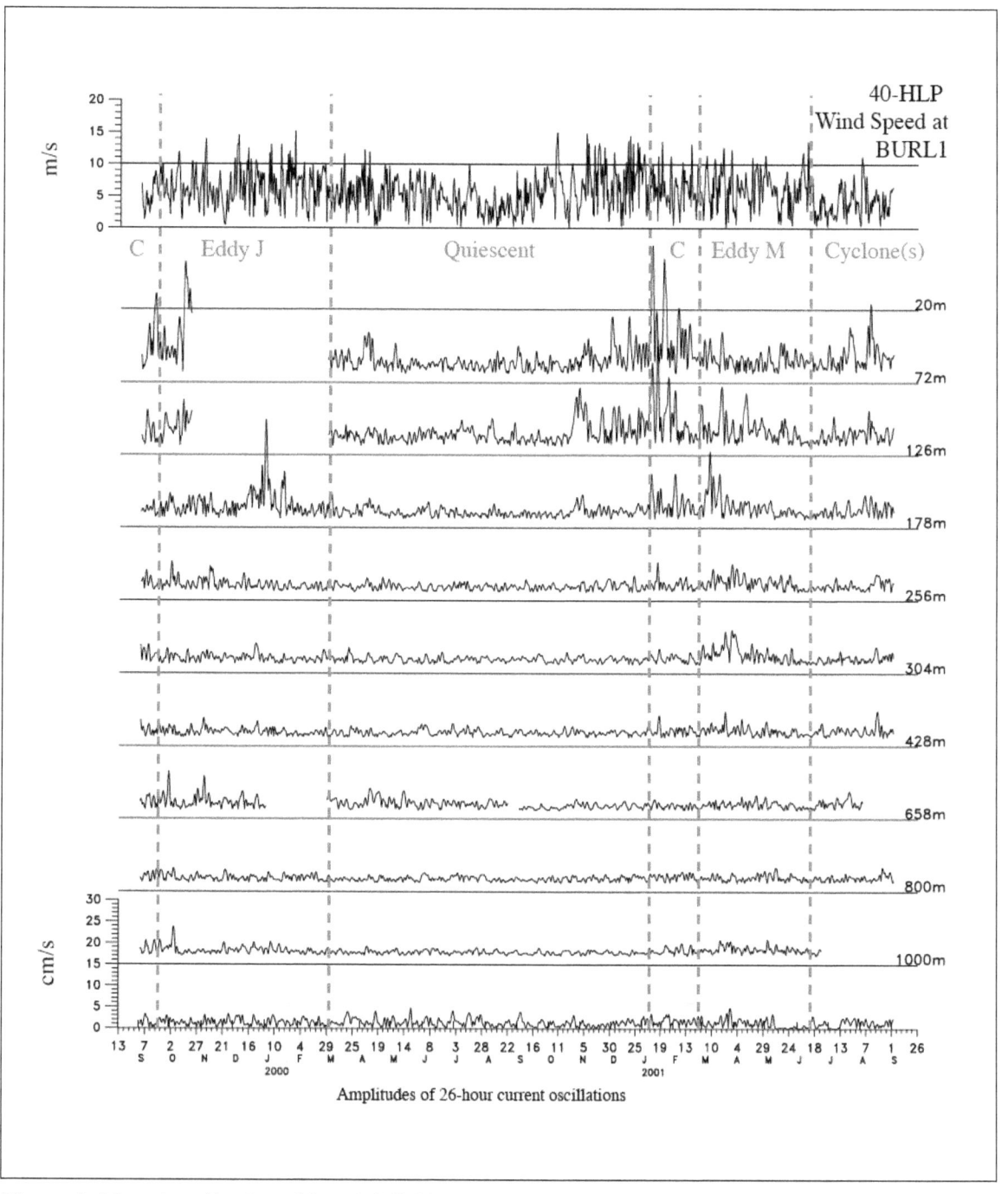

Figure 3-19. Amplitudes of inertial (26 hour) current oscillations at the indicated depths of mooring I1. Top panel shows the 40-HLP wind speed at the BURL1 C-MAN Station. Vertical lines show intervals when LC eddies and their peripheral cyclones (C) dominate the upper layer at the site.

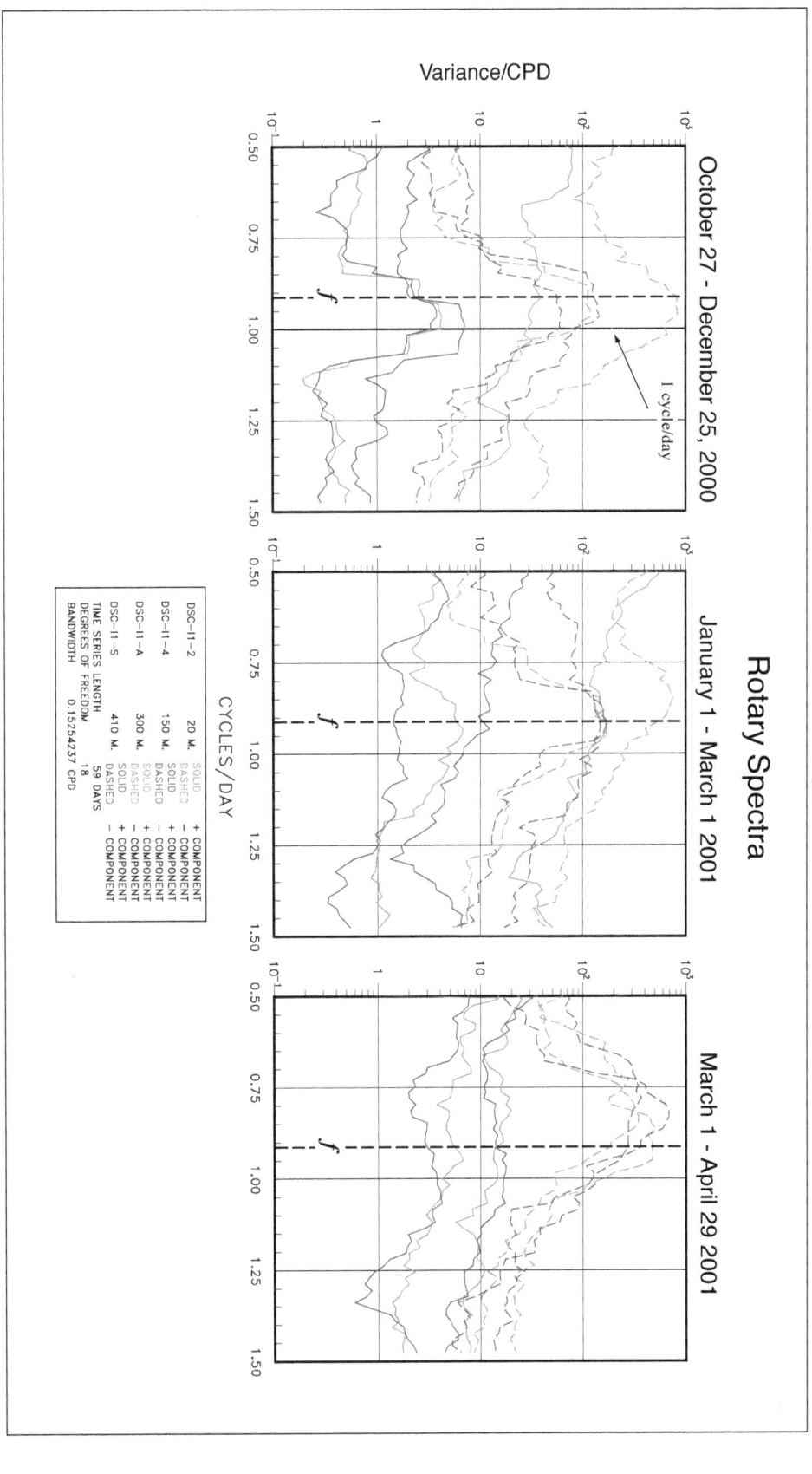

Figure 3-20. Rotary spectra (clockwise - dashed, anticlockwise - solid) for the indicated upper layer current records for three 59-day periods. The inertial frequency, f, at I1 is indicated on the plots.

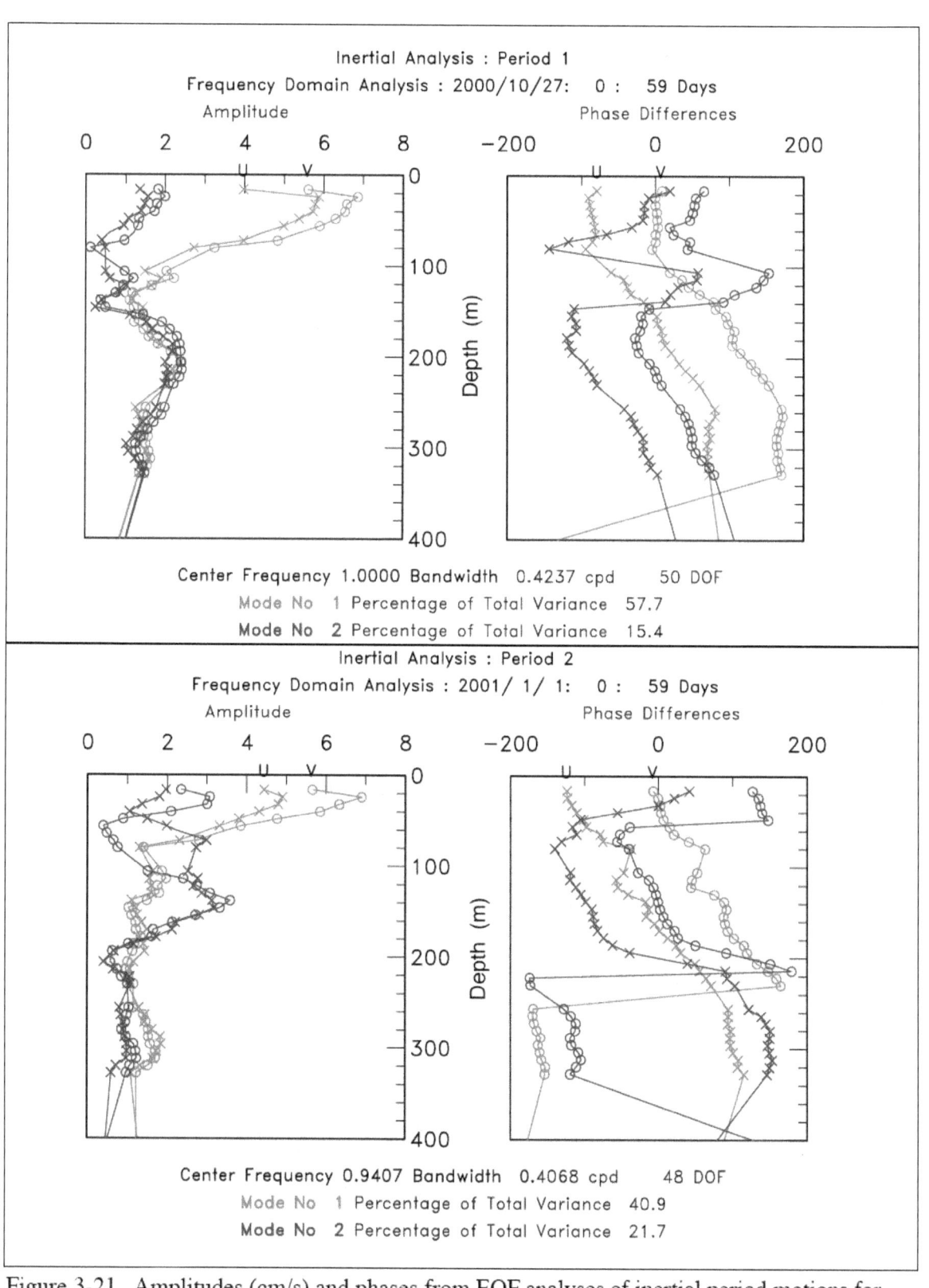

Figure 3-21. Amplitudes (cm/s) and phases from EOF analyses of inertial period motions for periods 1 (top) and 2 (bottom).

70

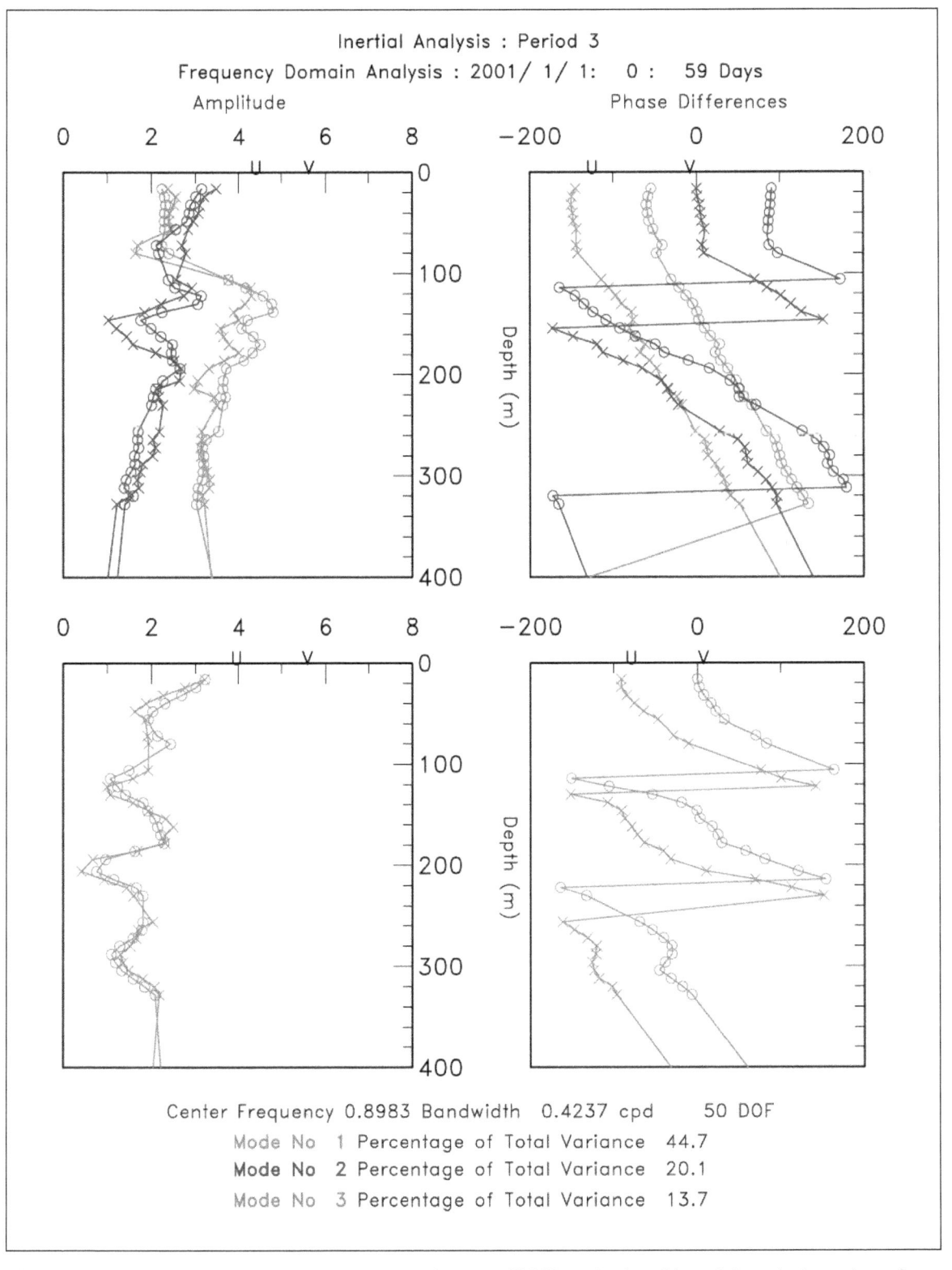

Figure 3-22. Amplitudes (cm/s) and phases from an EOF analysis of inertial period motions for period 3.

4.0 ECHO SOUNDERS WITH PRESSURE (PIES)

4.1 Introduction

For the final six months (nominally February through August 2001) of this extended set of DeSoto Canyon measurements, the MMS supplemented support from BP to extend the mooring at I1 to the full water column depth and to support placement of three PIES in a triangle around this full-depth mooring. The support to extend Mooring I1 to full depth was to help provide information that may provide additional insight about linkage of upper and lower layer current patterns. The PIES were used to provide an independent estimate of the vertical profiles of temperature salinity and hence density and geostrophic velocities. Placement of three PIES around the instrumented mooring provides a basis for comparing velocity and temperatures as estimated by the PIES and GEM methodology with nearby actual Eulerian current/temperature measurements made at various depths below the sea surface.

4.2   Methodology

4.2.1   Instrumentation

The Model 6.1 Inverted Echo Sounders (IES) deployed in the Gulf of Mexico is a bottom-mounted instrument that measures the vertical acoustic travel time (VATT) round-trip from the sea floor to the sea surface and back. The Model 6.1E used in this study (Figure 4-1) is a combined IES, data-logger and acoustic release, with bottom pressure and temperature measurements. From its position on the seafloor, the upward directed transducer at the top of the instrument (Figure 4-2), transmits a burst of four 10kHz acoustic pulses every 10 minutes. The time (τ or tau) required for the round trip from the instrument, to the water surface and back to the instrument is recorded internally. Pressure and temperature are also measured and recorded at 10-minute intervals (six/hour).

Features of the PIES: (See Figure 4-2)

- Entirely self-contained in a single, non-eroding, glass sphere: acoustic & timed release, flotation buoyancy and optional recovery aids (radio beacon, xenon flasher and flag)
- 32-bit microcontroller combines high-performance data manipulation with low-power operation modes.
- Data stored on removable (type ATA compact flash) memory cards (16-512Mbyte capacity)
- Data stored as engineering units n MS-DOS file formats
- Many self-test features
- "Through-the-glass" communications - high speed data download without opening the instrument housing
- Acoustic command subsystem, including data telemetry option

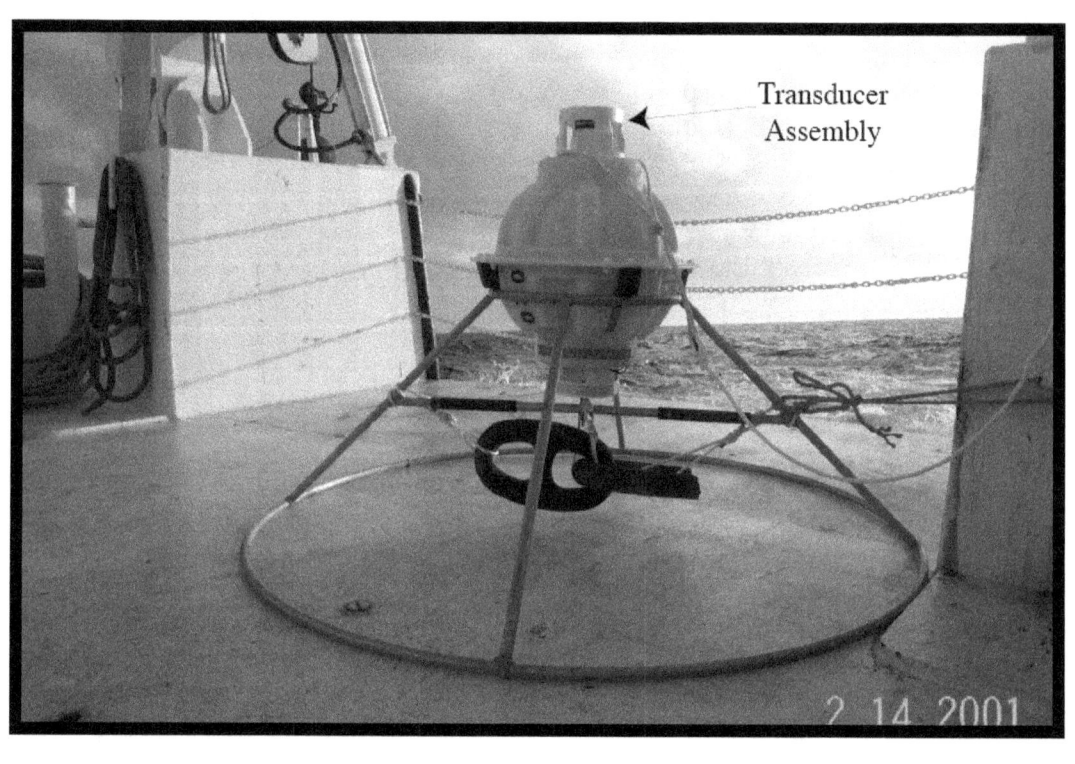

Figure 4-1. PIES on the back deck of the deployment vessel in a cradle used in regions of expected strong bottom currents. Prior to deployment, the ropes to the weights (chain links) were removed, as were the rubber "stoppers" around the equatorial rib. This configuration orients vertically on a sloping bottom since the weights tend to orient the instrument toward the vertical. The transducer is at the top of the sphere in this picture, and the release, radio and light are at the bottom. When the acoustic release is activated, the unit seperates from the chain links and the rises to the surface with the transducer pointing downward. This causes the light and radio to be at the water surface.

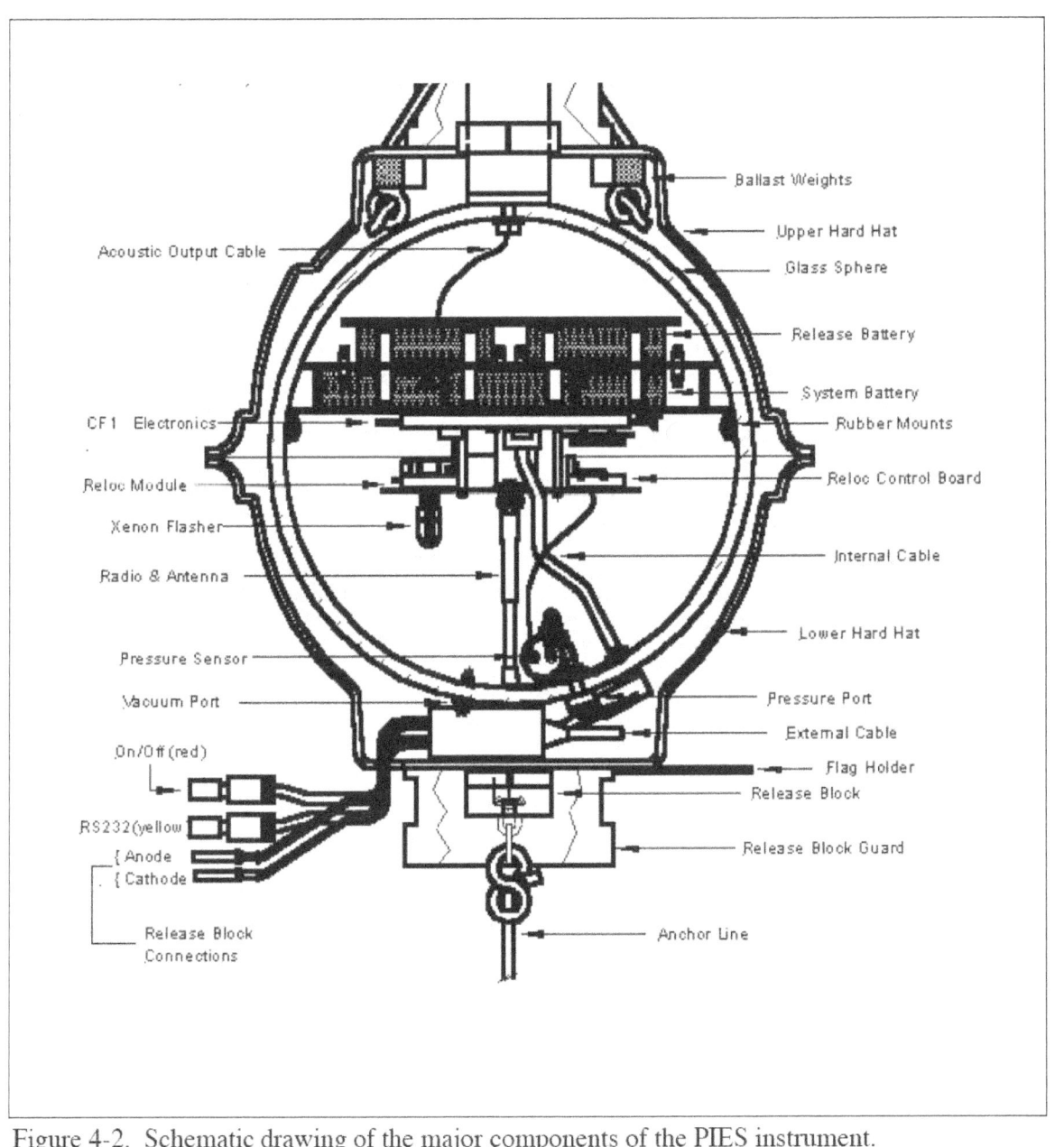

Figure 4-2. Schematic drawing of the major components of the PIES instrument.

- Acoustic command and data logging circuitry and batteries are independent

- 17-inch (43 cm) diameter glass-sphere instrument housing provides buoyancy for 120 or 180 Amp-Hr Lithium battery. Typical deployment durations of 2-5 years, depending on measurement schedule, water depth (output power) and battery capacity.

- Pressure/temperature sensors

- Long-term stability and barotropic pressure resolution better than $10\mu Pa$ - 0.1 mbar (equivalent to 0.001 m water)

The IES processes 24 individual echo measurements to produce a single travel time. In a typical deep-sea experiment, the ocean acoustic travel time sensitivity to changes in actual water surface height is about +1.3 milliseconds/meter (ms/m) with thermocline depth variations changing the travel time by approximately 0.05 ms/m.

To eliminate early echoes from reverberation and false targets, the IES echo detector is disabled immediately after the acoustic transmission for a period of time called the *lockout time*. The detector is enabled again just before the anticipated surface echo. To minimize false echoes from fish and other weak targets, the IES acoustic *output power level* is adjusted for depth under firmware control so that the sea surface is the most viable target. The optimal lockout time and output power level are suggested by the IES firmware after the user estimates the deployment depth. This setting can be overridden/set manually by the user.

An IES equipped for pressure measurements (PIES) uses a quartz sensor made by Paroscientific, Inc. for high accuracy and resolution. Paroscientific's stated accuracy of 0.01% for this line of sensor is well established. Typical resolution of Paros sensors is better than 1 part per million, and under stabilized conditions, resolution can approach 1 part per billion. In the typical PIES application, where the temperature and pressure are changing slowly and are relatively stable, the estimated sensor resolution is one part in 10 million. In the PIES, the pressure channel electronics measure with a resolution of about 1:64,000,000; that's about 0.00016 lbs/inch^2 (psi) or about 0.16 mm H$_2$O for a 10,000 psi sensor. This ensures that the PIES pressure measurement resolution is limited by the capabilities of the sensor and not by the PIES electronic circuits.

4.2.2 Initial Data Conditioning

The IES internally processed 24 individual echo measurements to produce a single travel time (one averaged travel time per hour, i.e. four echos per 10-minute interval averaged over six 10-minute intervals). In a typical deep-sea experiment, the ocean acoustic travel time sensitivity to changes in actual water surface height is about +1.3 milliseconds/meter (ms/m) with thermocline depth variations changing the travel time by approximately 0.05 ms/m. Any obvious spikes in the hourly records were replaced with interpolated values during subsequent data quality control. Processing of the pressure measurements included removing spikes, long-term drifts and the tides. Tidal response analysis (Munk and Cartwright, 1965) was used to determine the tidal constituents for each record. Long-term drifts were identified by fitting exponential-linear curves in a least-squares sense to the detided pressure records. The travel time, pressure and temperature records were low-pass filtered using a second-order Butterworth filter with a cutoff period of 40 hours. The filter was passed forward and backward in time to avoid introducing phase shifts. Twenty hours of data at each end of the filtered series were discarded to avoid startup transients. After filtering all time series were subsampled at 12-hour intervals.

4.2.3 Data Processing and Reduction – Gravest Empirical Mode

In the present experiment, an empirical relationship has been established between $\tau_{100\text{-}1000}$, round trip travel time between 100 and 1000 dbar surfaces, and vertical profiles of temperature, salinity, and specific volume anomaly using historical hydrography, the so-called Gravest Empirical Mode (GEM) representation (e.g., Meinen and Watts, 2000 and Watts et al., 2001)

For the GEM construction in the present study, we utilized 446 hydrographic stations from the Gulf of Mexico HYDRO Database compiled by TAMU as part of MMS-funded Deepwater Reanalysis as well as additional stations provided by SAIC. Due to the integral nature of τ and the fact that this study represents an initial attempt to establish a GEM field for the Gulf of Mexico, only high vertical resolution CTD hydrocasts were retained in the analysis. The spatial and temporal distribution of these hydrocasts are shown in Figure 4-3. The northwestern Gulf of Mexico is well sampled; hydrocasts represent about 20 years of sampling; hydrocasts sample most the annual cycle, except December; the bulk of casts extend between 1000 to 2000 dbar with relatively few cast below 2000 dbar.

The upper limit of the τ (tau) integration was chosen as 100 dbar in an effort to avoid the influence of the seasonal cycle; the bulk of the 'contamination' of τ from seasonal variability should be above the mixed layer. In the future, further refinement to the GEM field will include a seasonal correction (e.g., Watts et al., 2001). The lower limit of the τ integration was chosen as 1000 dbar in an effort to balance two needs: extend the integration below the thermocline and retain as many of the acquired historical hydrocasts as possible.

The GEM field was determined as follows. First, the historical hydrocasts were linearly interpolated to a uniform 25 dbar grid. Second, for every 25 dbar, a cubic smoothing spline was fitted to the temperature measurements as a function of $\tau_{100\text{-}1000}$. The same procedure was applied to salinity and specific volume anomaly. Figures 4-4, 4-5, and 4-6 illustrate this fit for several pressure surfaces. Root-mean-square residual, rms, for each curve provides an indication of the departure any individual profile might have from the GEM curve. The rms values for temperature, salinity, and specific volume anomaly are small and decrease with increasing pressure (depth). The curves show that a functional relationship exists between the integrated variable $\tau_{100\text{-}1000}$ and vertical profiles of temperature, salinity, and specific volume anomaly. Figures 4-7 and 4-8 show contours of the temperature and salinity fits for all pressure surfaces as a function of $\tau_{100\text{-}1000}$, the two-dimensional ``GEM fields." Note the lack of deep casts (> 2000 dbar) for $\tau_{100\text{-}1000}$ less than about 1.188 s. There is little structure in the temperature and salinity GEM fields below about 1000 dbars and this reflects the uniform deep water properties observed on the Gulf of Mexico. The GEM field provides a look-up table; given a $\tau_{100\text{-}1000}$ value, profiles of temperature, salinity, and specific volume anomaly can be determined.

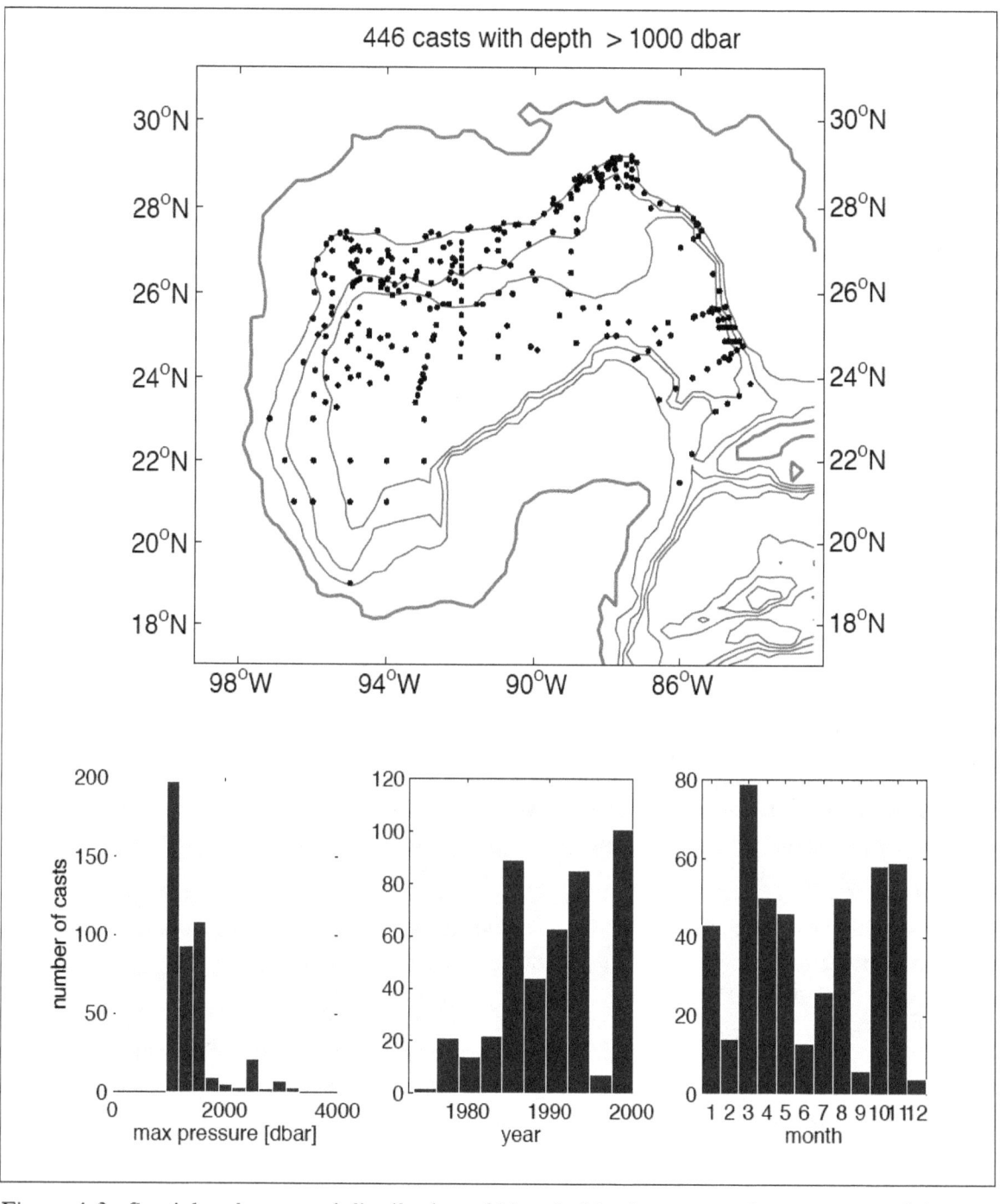

Figure 4-3. Spatial and temporal distribution of historical hydrocasts used to construct of the Gravest Empirical Mode. Data provided by the Gulf of Mexico HYDRO Database compiled by TAMU as part of the MMS-funded Deepwater Reanalysis and additional stations provided by SAIC. Top panel. Spatial distribution of the hydrocasts with bathymetry contoured every 1000 m. Histograms of the maximum hydrocast pressure (bottom left), year of hydrocast (middle), and month of hydrocast (right).

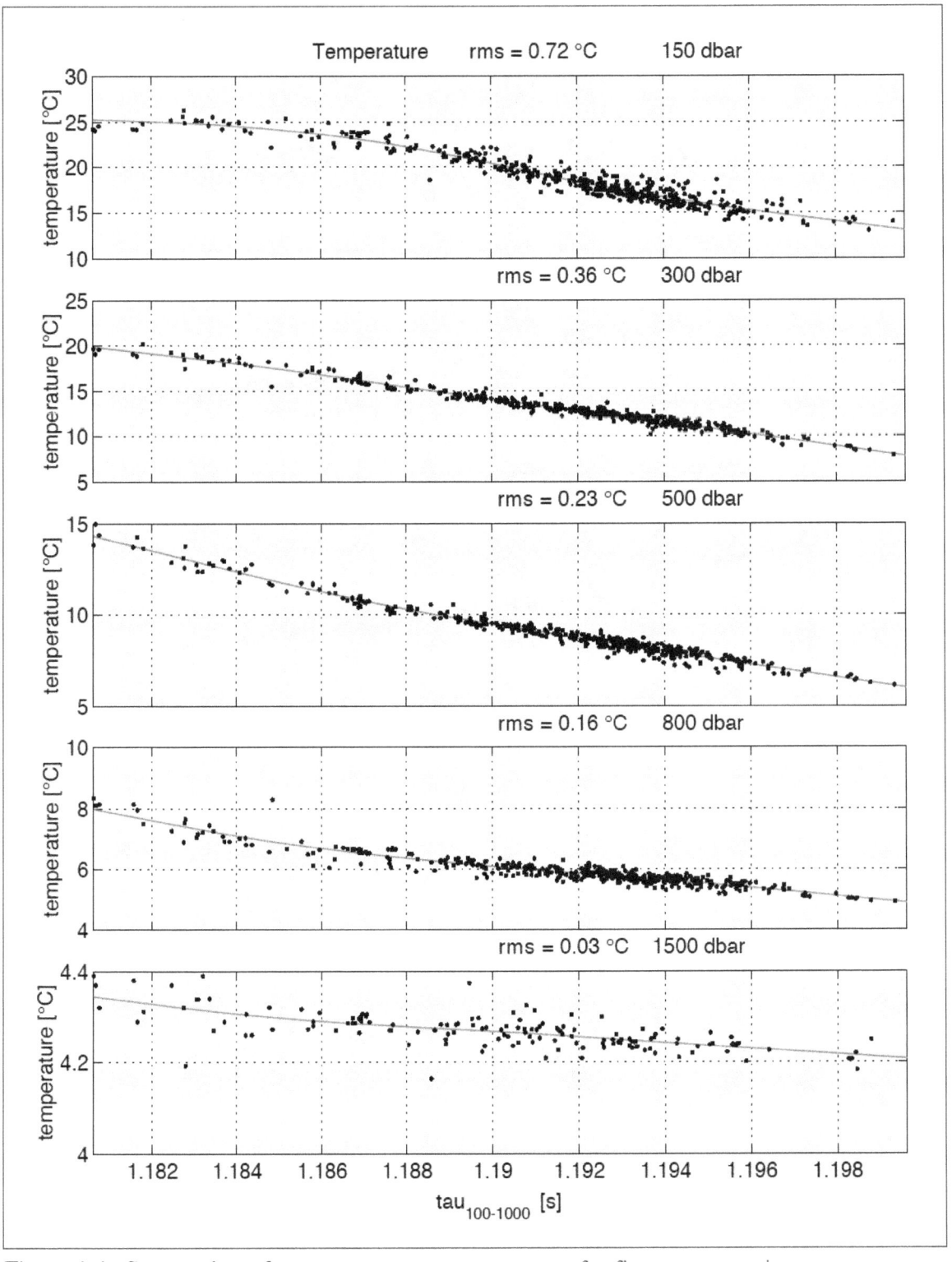

Figure 4-4. Scatter plots of temperature versus $tau_{100-1000}$ for five representative pressure levels. At each pressure, the temperature versus $tau_{100-1000}$ data are fitted by a cubic smoothing spline (solid curve).

79

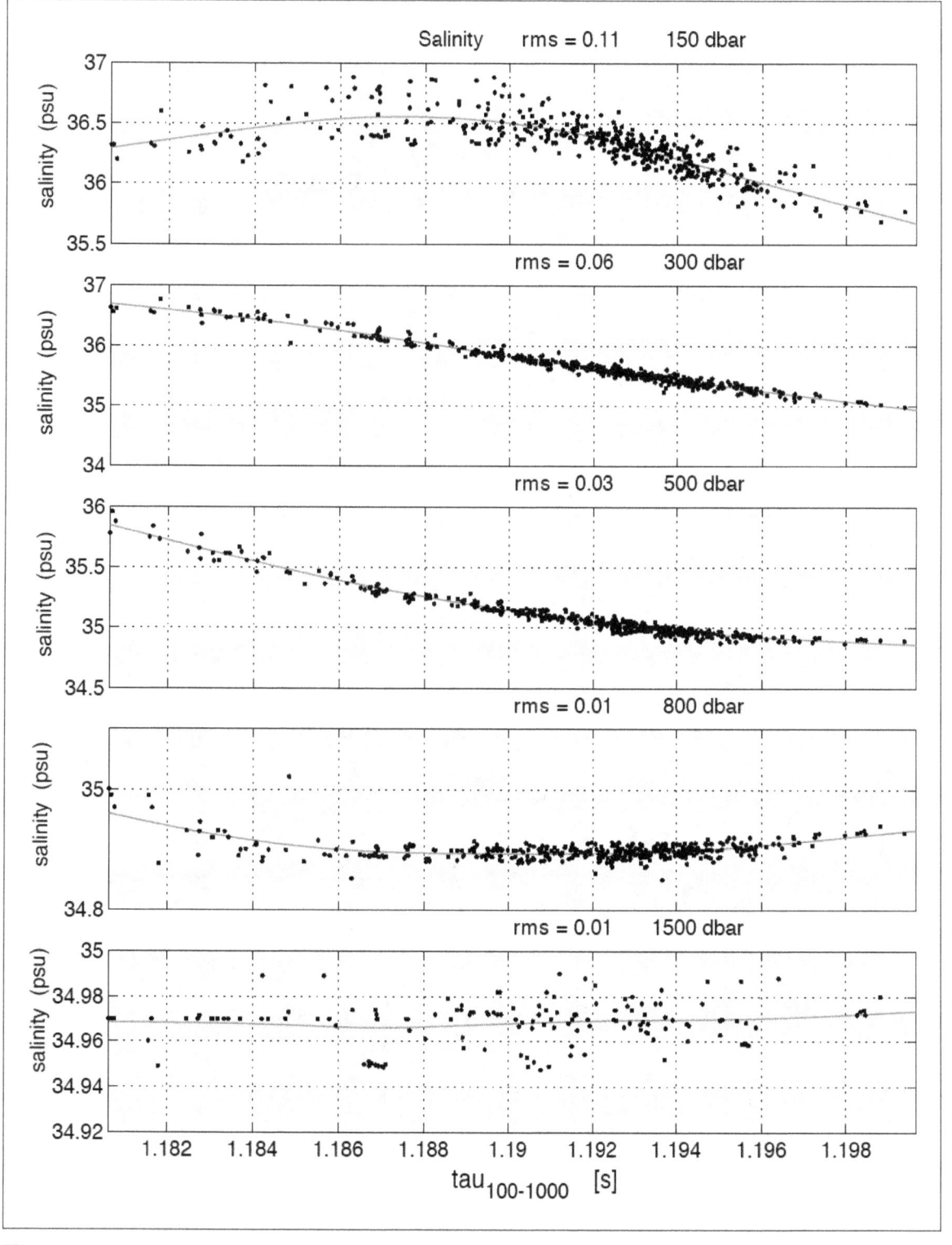

Figure 4-5. Scatter plots of salinity versus $tau_{100-1000}$ for five representative pressure levels. At each pressure, the salinity versus $tau_{100-1000}$ data are fitted by a cubic smoothing spline (solid curve).

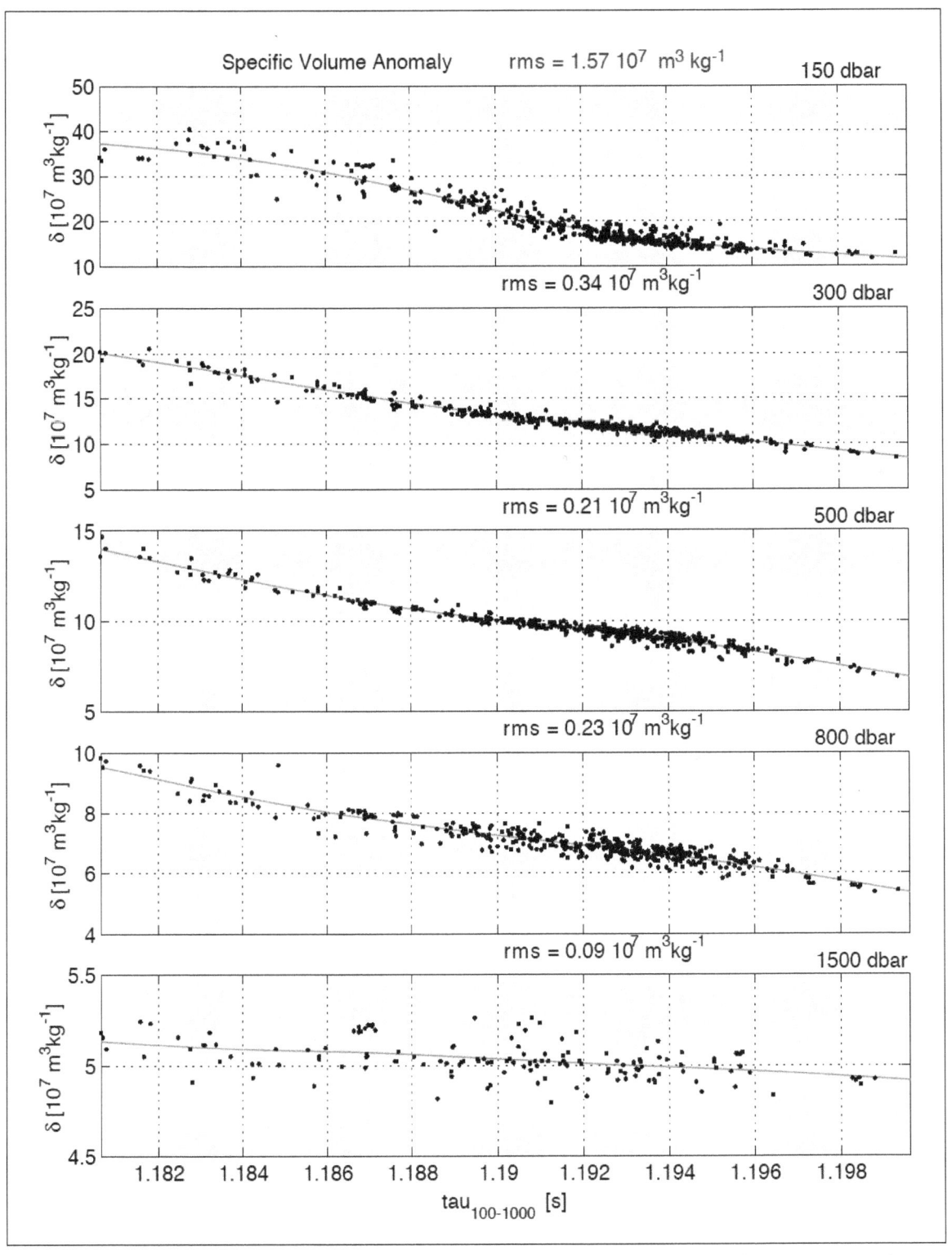

Figure 4-6. Scatter plots of specific volume anomaly versus $tau_{100\text{-}1000}$ for five representative pressure levels. At each pressure, the specific volume anomaly versus $tau_{100\text{-}1000}$ data are fitted by a cubic smoothing spline (solid curve).

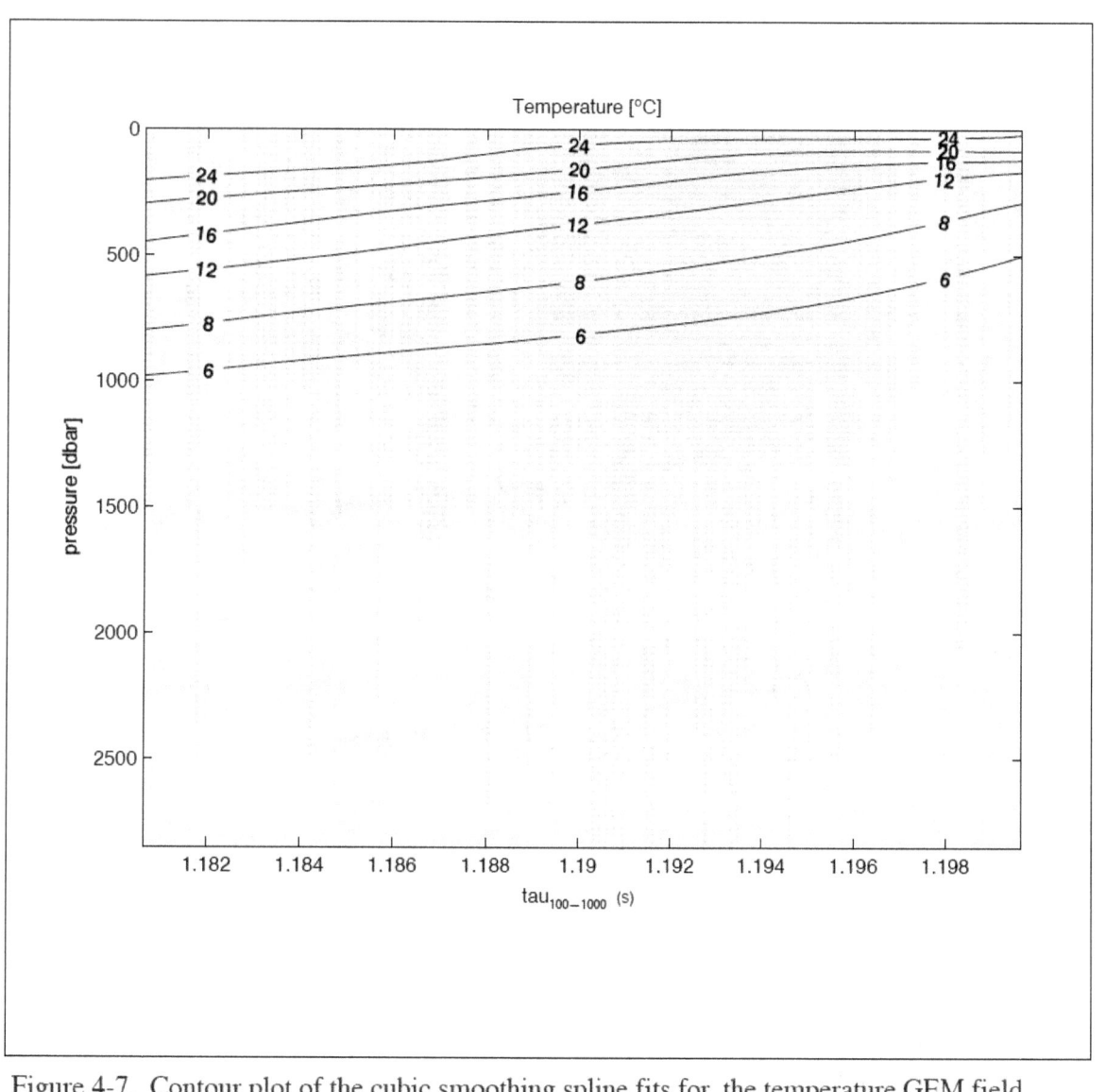

Figure 4-7. Contour plot of the cubic smoothing spline fits for the temperature GEM field.
Grey dots indicate positions of CTD data.

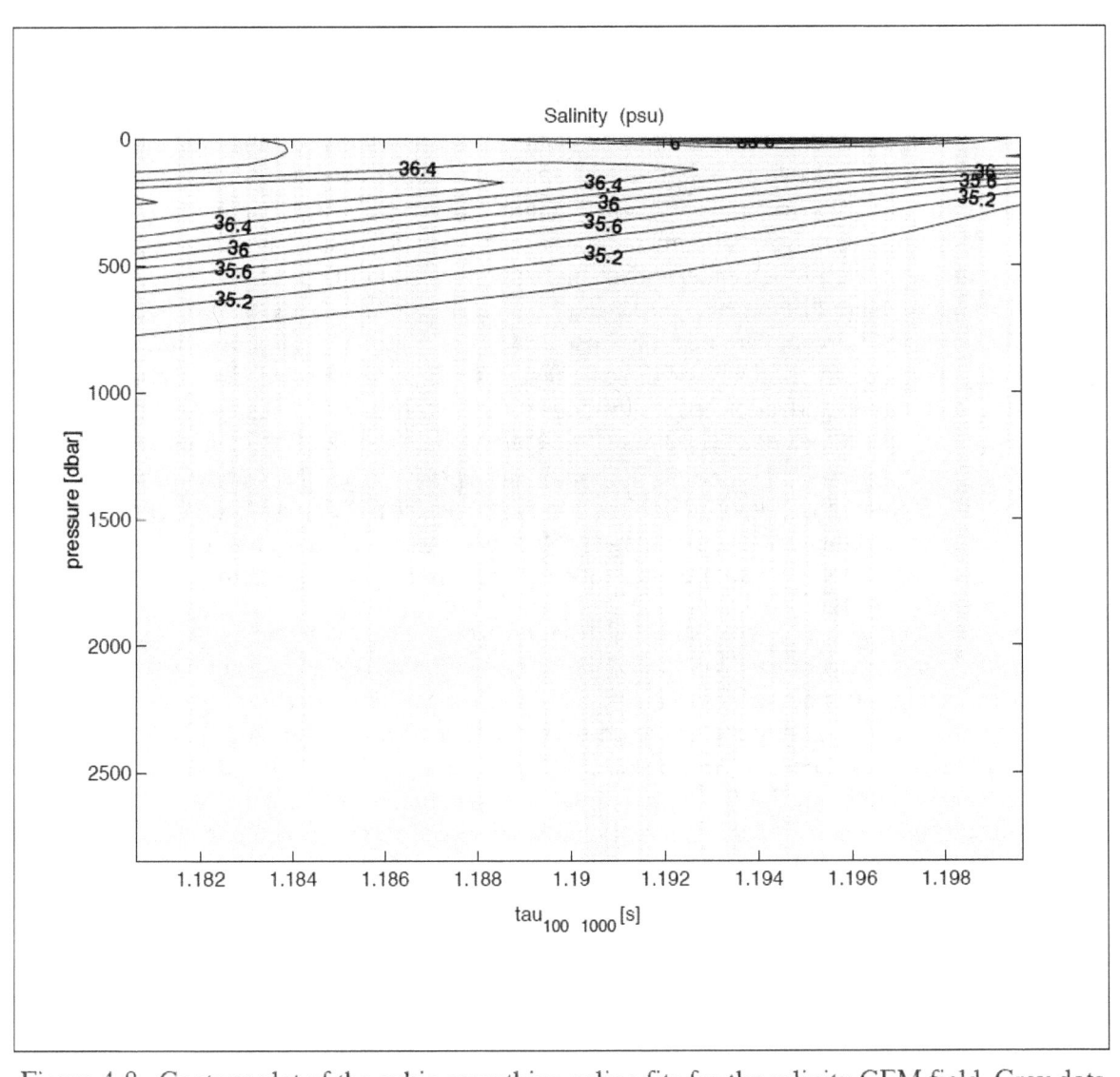

Figure 4-8. Contour plot of the cubic smoothing spline fits for the salinity GEM field. Grey dots indicate the positions of CTD data.

4.3   PIES in the Gulf of Mexico

The tau (τ) time series measured by the three Gulf of Mexico PIES were calibrated to $\tau_{100\text{-}1000}$ as described by Meinen and Watts (1998). For each $\tau_{100\text{-}1000}$ the GEM parameterizations provide look-up tables for temperature, salinity, and specific volume anomaly for any pressure; the calibrated τ times series from the 3 PIES combined with the GEM parameterization yields estimates of vertical profiles of temperature, salinity, and specific volume anomaly. These estimates compared well to the independent measurements from the nearby I1 mooring (Figure 4-9). RMS temperature differences range from 1.3°C at 150 dbar to 0.5°C at 650 dbar (Figure 4-10); RMS salinity differences are near 0.08 psu at 450 dbar (Figure 4-11). The time series have been weekly averaged to eliminate small-scale features. These differences derive not only from instrument and parameterization errors but also reflect horizontal density gradients as the instruments are not co-located. The largest differences between the PIES temperature records occur in the early part of the record (February through June) as the Loop Current extends northward to 27°N and the Eddy Millennium forms and detaches from the Loop Current. At that time upper-ocean velocities were strong (>50 cm/s, upper right panel of Figure 4-12); corresponding horizontal temperature gradients were necessarily large (geostrophy).

Geostrophic velocity shears were estimated from horizontal density gradients. Again, density at any pressure can be determined via the GEM parameterization. These shears were referenced with either deep geostrophic velocity calculated from the near-bottom pressure gauges (Figure 4-12) or with the deepest current meter record from the I1 mooring (Figure 4-13) Note equipment failures of the pressure sensors for a portion of the deployment have reduced the time series to span late April through mid July. The triangular configuration of the PIES (a 2-D array) permits the estimate of the velocity vector (i.e., zonal and meridional velocity components). Comparison between the PIES estimated velocities referenced with the deep geostrophic velocities to the directly-measured velocity records reveals RMS velocity differences near 7 cm/s at 120 dbar and 5 cm/s at 1980 dbar (Figure 4-12). Note that the bottom left panel in Figure 4-12 shows the geostrophic velocity determined solely from deep pressure gauge while the bottom panels in Figure 4-13 is the deepest current meter record from the I1 mooring. Although the weekly averaging of the time series greatly reduces the amplitude of small-scale features, part of the discrepancy may be attributed to the fact that the mooring velocities are point measurements and the PIES velocities are geostrophic, and hence, represent the average velocity between the PIES. The comparison is encouraging in several aspects: the upper-ocean velocity vectors illustrate the strong currents associated with the Loop Current and Loop Current Eddy detachment and the deep velocity vectors show the strong current pulses as topographic Rossby waves pass through the mooring.

4.4   Conclusion

Although refinements may be made to the Gulf of Mexico GEM parameterization with future availability of additional appropriate hydrographic profiles, the present analysis illustrates that a robust empirical relationship exists between τ (tau) and vertical profiles of salinity, temperature and density. A two-dimensional array of PIES will provide the basis for estimating a time series of vertical profiles of the geostrophic velocity vector that can be referenced by measured deep velocities. The comparison of PIES-based velocity estimates and measured velocities was good.

84

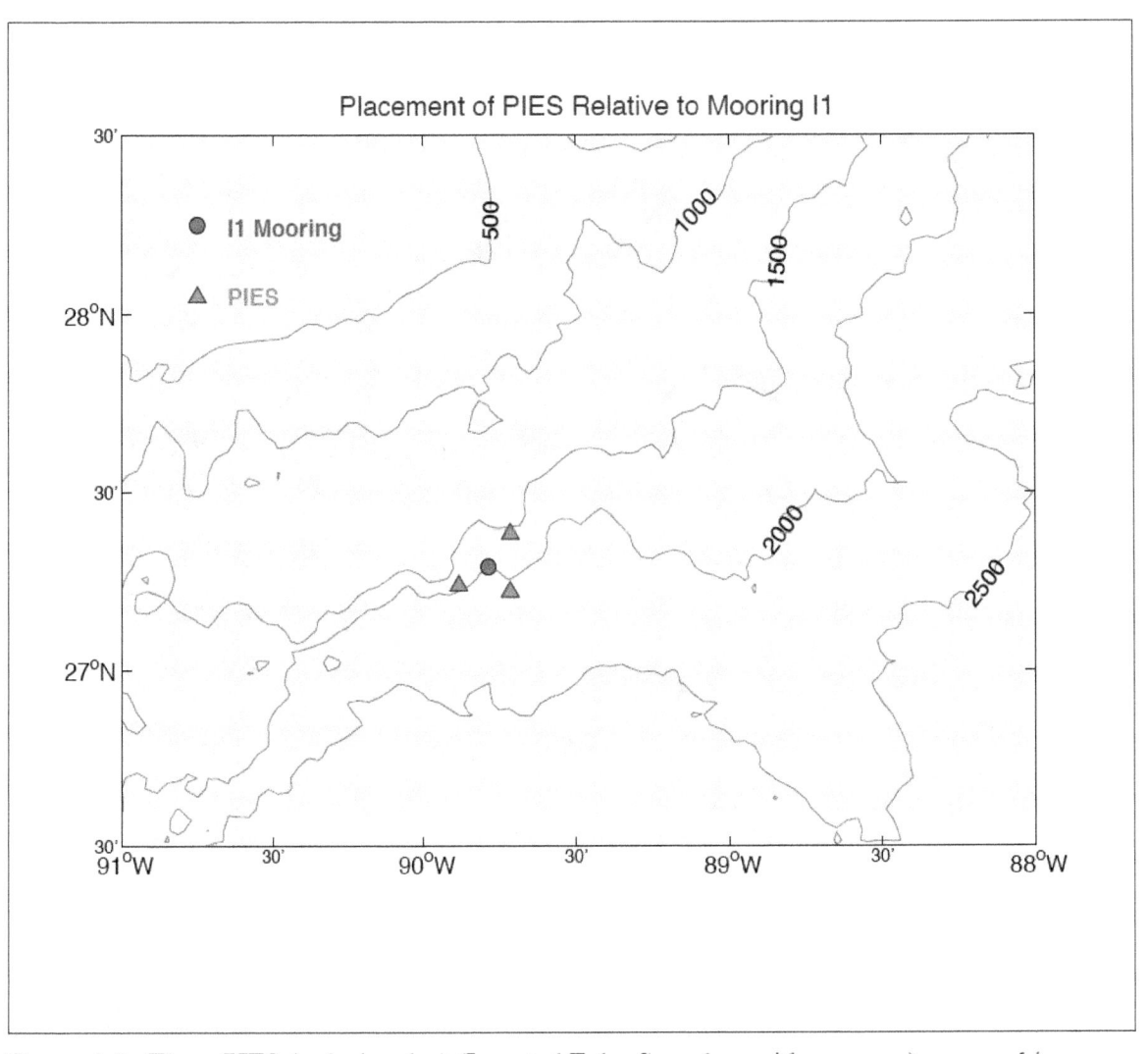

Figure 4-9. Three PIES (red triangles) (Inverted Echo Sounders with pressure) arranged in a triangle around the I1 mooring (circle) for approximately 6 months, February through August 2001. Bathymetry is contoured every 500 m.

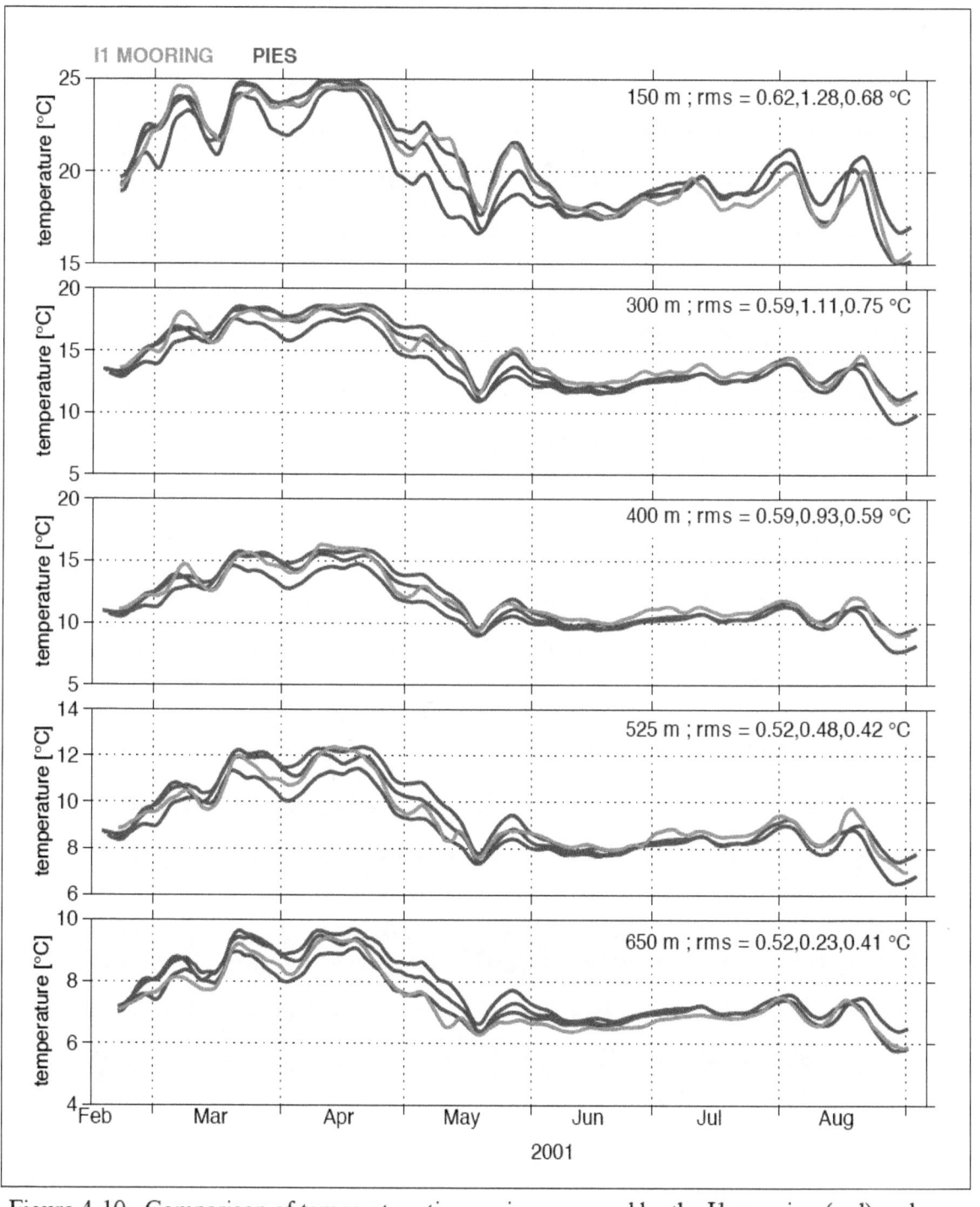

Figure 4-10. Comparison of temperature time series measured by the I1 mooring (red) and temperatures estimated at the same set of depths by the 3 nearby PIES (blue) using the GEM interpretation of the tau (τ) measurements.

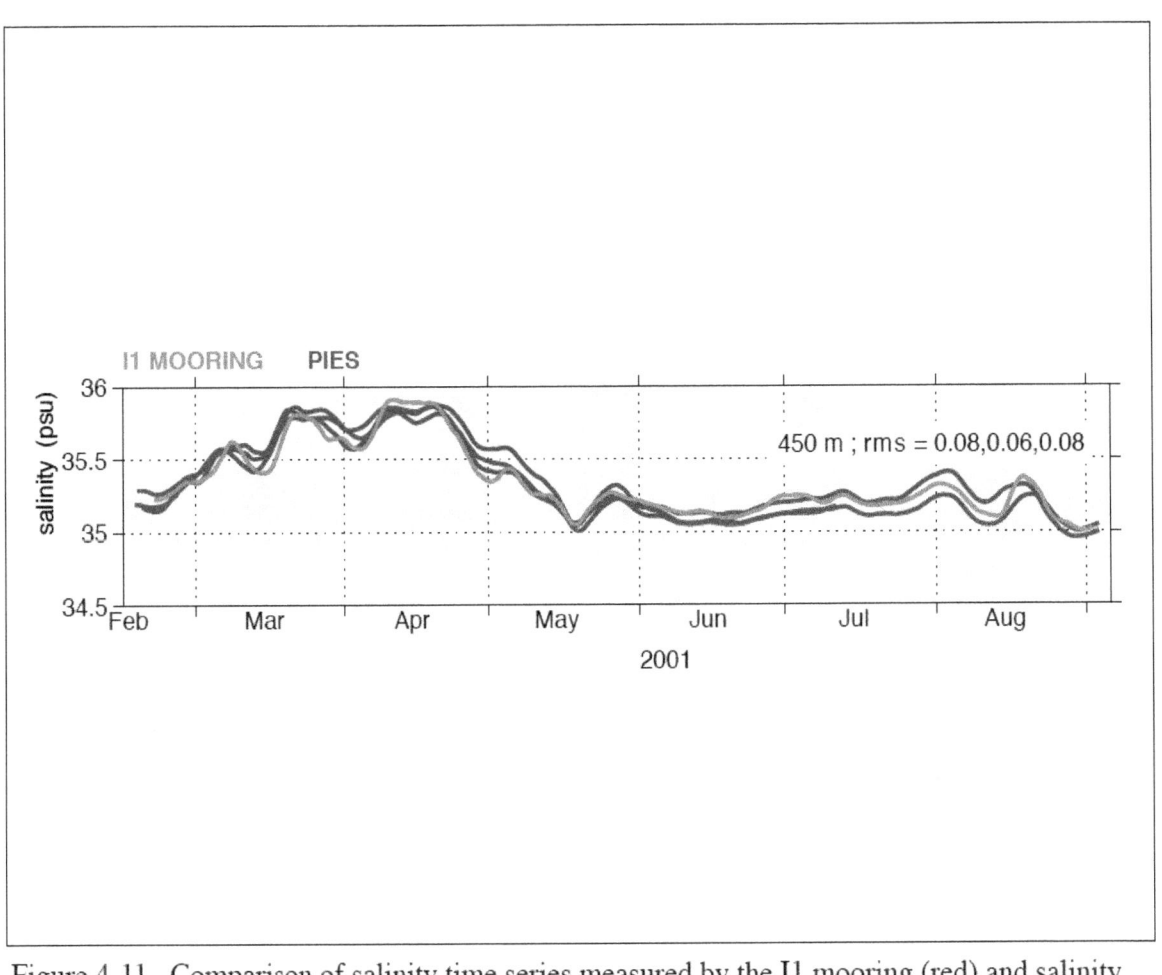

Figure 4-11. Comparison of salinity time series measured by the I1 mooring (red) and salinity estimated at 450 dbar by the 3 nearby PIES (blue) using the GEM interpretation of the tau (τ) measurements.

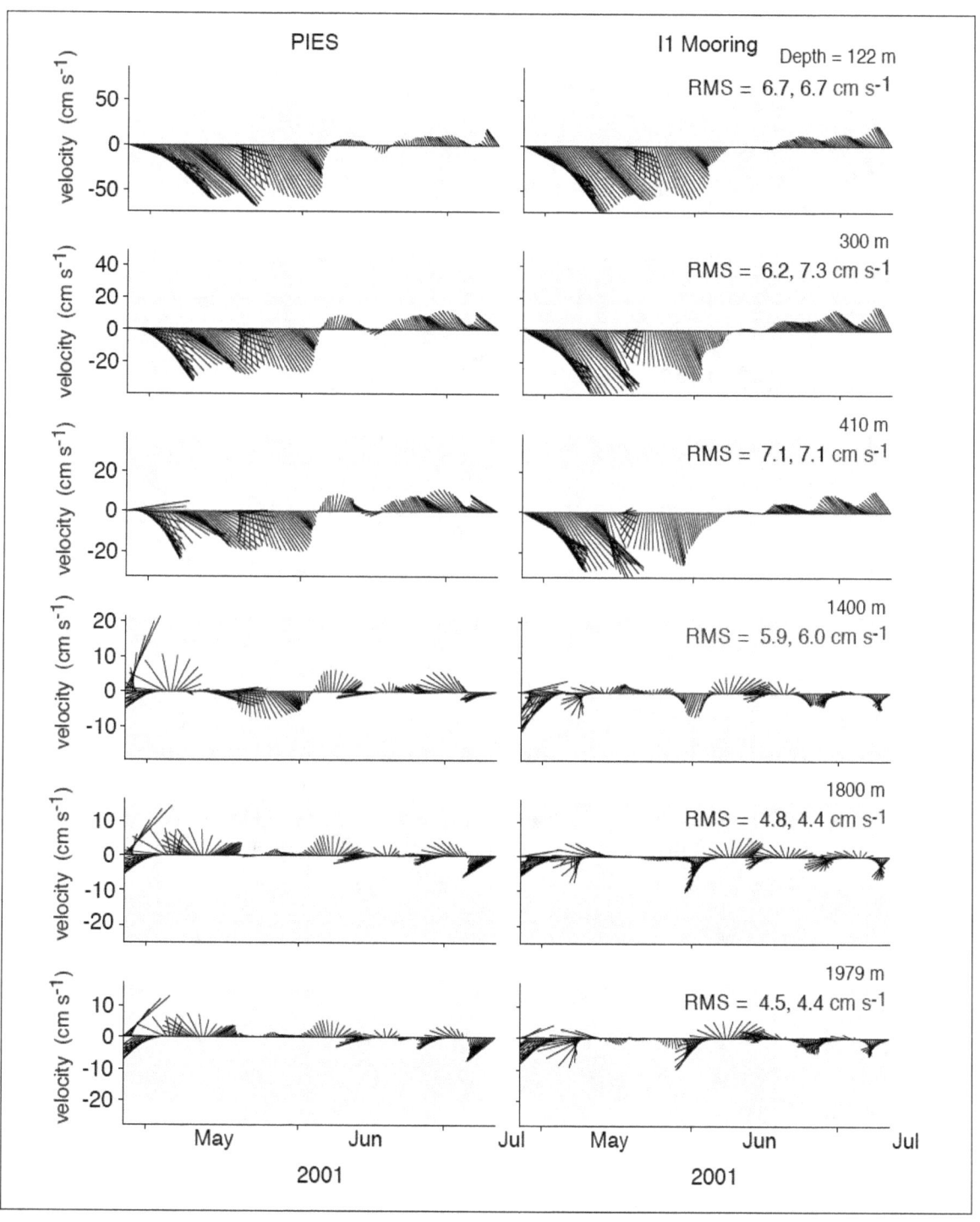

Figure 4-12. Comparison of velocity measured by the I1 mooring (right) and velocity estimated at the same set of depths by the 3 nearby PIES (left) using the GEM interpretation of the tau (τ) measurements and referencing geostrophic shears to deep geostrophic velocity determined from the bottom pressure measurements.

88

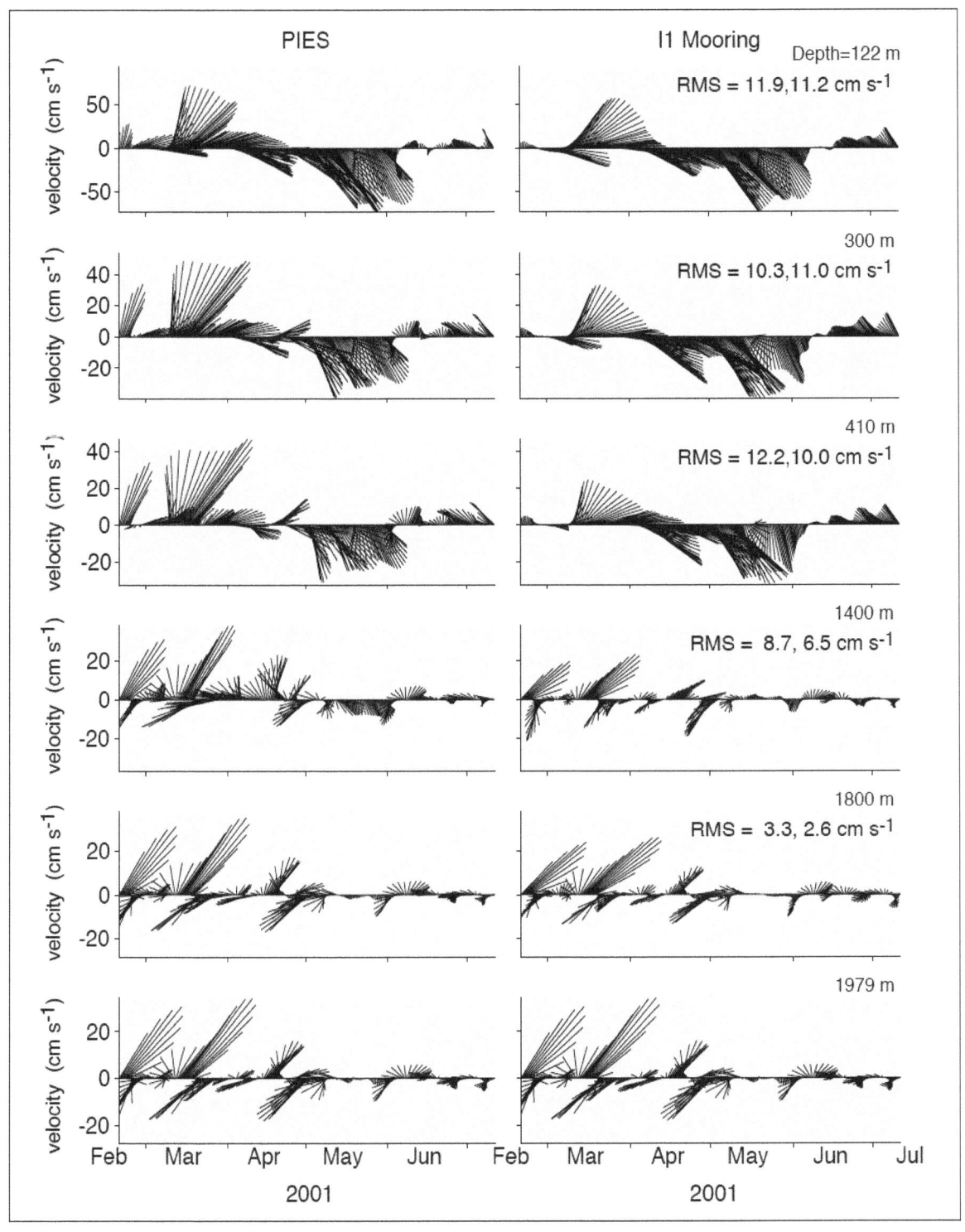

Figure 4-13. Comparison of velocity measured by the I1 mooring (right) and velocity estimated at the same set of depths by the 3 nearby PIES (left) using the GEM interpretation of the tau (τ) measurements and referencing geostrophic shears to the deep current meter on the I1 mooring.

5.0 SUMMARY

The two-years of data, from the three main moorings in the region of the Sigsbee Escarpment on the lower slope south of the Mississippi Delta, have shown unusual deep current flows. The bottom intensified, nearly depth-independent motions are typical of topgraphic Rossby waves observed in this and other regions of the deep Gulf. However, energy levels are exceptional and the dominant periods of the motions are about 10 to 14 days and short compared to other regions of the eastern and western Gulf (Hamilton, 1990). Maximum currents at the I2 mooring were of order 85 to 95 cm/s for an event early in the record. This energy seems to spill over the escarpment to the BP J1 site at the top of the Escarpment on some occasions when very-high energy events occurred at I2. Otherwise, the velocities at J1 were much less energetic than at the moorings south of the Escarpment. Similarly, bottom velocities at another site (I4), just west of I2, on the Escarpment, were also much weaker than measured at the base of the escarpment, and in deeper water depths.

The records show a number of distinct wave trains passing through the site. The first, between September 1999 and January 2000, showed the highest current speeds and at the beginning of the record there were indications that upper-layer disturbances, caused by cyclonic frontal eddies on the LC front, were coherent with the lower layer flows. In this first period, upper-layer currents were vigorous due to the presence of the LC and later, the recently shed eddy J. The second period began in April 2000 and lasted to the end of the record in August 2000. These TRW's were also energetic though with slightly longer characteristic periods, stronger bottom trapping, and larger westward amplification between I1 and I2, than observed in the first period. The upper layer currents were quiescent during this second period as Eddy J had moved off into the western Gulf. Thus, there was no evident connection with the initiation of the April TRW's with simultaneous fluctuations of the upper-layer currents. A third interval of energetic TRW's, beginning in February 2001, was associated with the shedding of Eddy M and associated cyclonic circulations. In all, five wave trains, with differing periods and wavelengths were identified in the bottom records. Ray-tracing suggests that the west side of the LC is the most likely source region for these waves and that it is difficult for such short period waves to penetrate into the western Gulf basin. This is an accord with earlier measurements (Hamilton 1990) that showed 20 to 30 day TRW's dominating in the central and western Gulf. If the mechanism for coupling of surface propagating eddies or meanders with deep TRW motions that has been put forward for TRW generation by the Gulf Stream in the North Atlantic (Pickart, 1995) applies here, then small cyclonic frontal eddies on the LC and LCE fronts could be candidates for generating deep, short-period TRW's in the eastern Gulf.

It is apparent from these measurements and the previous one-year of current data obtained by BP at a site close to I1 (Hamilton, 1998), that TRW activity is fairly continuous at the base of the escarpment in this region. The distribution of energy across the array was quite inhomogeneous, and varied with the different observed wave trains. The rotation of the principal axes of the motions from partly across-isobath at I3 to along-isobath at I1 and I2 suggests that the steep escarpment may be influencing the propagation of the TRW's, possibly by reflecting the energy back into deep water. The weak currents at J1 and I4 suggest that it is an effective barrier to TRW motions propagating into shallower water.

Upper layer currents were dominated by the passage of the two major LC anticyclones. The periphery of these eddies seem to have produced the most energetic temperature and velocity fluctuations that were often associated with rapidly translating cold cyclones. The passage of Eddy M into the western Gulf, between February and June 2001, allowed partial analysis of radial and azimuthal flows from mooring I1. This eddy moved further north than the previous Eddy J, and the center of the eddy passed within 60 km of the mooring, so that a substantial portion of the eddy interior was measured. The path and characteristics of the eddy were analyzed using drifters deployed by Horizon Marine. Eddy M was probably forced northwards and towards the slope by a large cyclone on its western side that formed while the eddy was still attached to the LC. This cyclone eventually moved up onto the slope and blocked further westward passage of Eddy M, which moved rapidly southwards during May 2001, and then resumed a more usual southwestward path into the western deep Gulf. The azimuthal velocity and temperature profiles behaved roughly as expected for an elliptical eddy in solid body rotation with a period of 8 to 10 days. However, there were significant anomalies that were associated with either attachment to the Loop Current or interactions with the cyclone and slope. The passage of the eddy allowed estimation of the distances from the center to the maximum velocity, along the semi-major axis, and the width of the cyclonic shear zone outside the maximum velocity position. These were 150 and 50 km, respectively. The narrow cyclonic shear zone implies a large positive vorticity anomaly and thus a generation region for non-linear instabilities.

Upper layer inertial currents were also analyzed. In the January – February, 2001 period, before the arrival of Eddy M, when the upper layer velocities were dominated by vigorous interacting cyclones, strong inertial currents were generated in the surface layer. These were more vigorous than in the fall and winter of 2000, when background currents were small and wind forcing was stronger. It was speculated that the interacting eddies were partially responsible for the increased amplitudes of the inertial oscillations. The January – February inertial waves did not propagate to deeper depths until Eddy M arrived. In Eddy M, the region just above the main thermocline had greater inertial energy than the surface indicating the propagating inertial internal waves were being trapped by the negative vorticity anomaly in the center of the eddy. Below 800 to 1000 m, inertial oscillations had negligible amplitudes.

This study deployed, around I1, three bottom-mounted PIES to test the viability of using the gravest empirical mode (GEM) method to generate low-frequency temperature, salinity and geostrophic velocity depth profiles. Deployment of an array of PIES and bottom current meter moorings is much more cost effective for large-scale measurement programs in deep water, than deploying arrays of full-depth moorings like I1. A preliminary GEM was constructed from historical CTD data for the Gulf and applied to the bottom pressure and travel time records from the three PIES deployed in the last 6-months of the study. The resulting derived profiles of temperature, salinity and geostrophic currents were compared with appropriate direct measurements of these quantities from mooring I1. The time series comparisons were good for all depths with high statistical significance and confidence. The last six months of the deployment included part of the passage of Eddy M. This work will allow the confident use of PIES in future deep Gulf physical oceanographic measurement programs.

6.0 REFERENCES

Berger, T., P. Hamilton, J.J. Singer, R.R. Leben, G.H. Born, and C.A. Fox. 1996. Louisiana/Texas shelf physical oceanography program: Eddy circulation study, final synthesis report. Vol 1: Technical Report. U.S. Dept. of the Interior, MMS, Gulf of Mexico OCS Region, New Orleans, LA. OCS Study MMS 96-0051.   324 pp.

Brooks, D.A. 1983. The wake of Hurricane Allen in the western Gulf of Mexico. Deep-Sea Res. 13: 117-129.

Chen, C., R.O. Reid, and W.D. Nowlin. 1996. Near-inertial oscillations over the Texas-Louisiana shelf. J. Geophys. Res. 101: 3509-3524.

Cooper, C.K., G.Z. Forristall, and T.M. Joyce. 1990. Velocity and hydrographic structure of two Gulf of Mexico warm-core rings. J. Geophys. Res. 95: 1663-1680.

Dierckx, P. 1982. A fast algorithm for smoothing data on a rectangular grid while using spline functions. SIAM J. Numer. Anal. 19: 1286-1304.

Elliot, B.A. 1982. Anticyclonic rings in the Gulf of Mexico. J. Phys. Oceanogr. 12:1292-1309.

Fields, E., K.L. Tracey, and D.R. Watts. 1991. Inverted echo sounder data processing report. University of Rhode Island-GSO Tech. Report 91-3. 1551 pp.

Foreman, M.G.G. 1979. Manual for tidal currents analysis and prediction. Pacific Marine Sci. Rep. 78-6, Institute of Ocean Studies, Patricia Bay, Sydney BC.   70 pp.

Glenn, S.M., G.Z. Forristall, P. Cornillon, and G. Milkowski. 1990. Observations of Gulf Stream ring 83-E and their interpretation using feature models. J. Geophys. Res. 98: 20,105-20,119.

Gonella, J. 1971. A local study of inertial oscillations in the upper layers of the ocean. Deep-Sea Res. 18: 775-788.

Hamilton, P. 1990. Deep currents in the Gulf of Mexico. J. Phys. Oceanogr. 20:1087-1104.

Hamilton, P. 1992. Lower continental slope cyclonic eddies in the central Gulf of Mexico. J. Geophys. Res. 97(C2): 2185-2200.

Hamilton, P. 1998. Analysis of Currents at the BP Atwater Valley Block 618 Exploration Site. SAIC Final Report, submitted to BP Exploration Inc.

Hamilton, P., G.S. Fargion, and D.C. Biggs. 1999. Loop Current eddy paths in the western Gulf of Mexico. J. Phys. Oceanogr. 29: 1180-1207.

Hamilton P., T.J. Berger, J.H. Churchill, R.R. Leben, T.N. Lee, J.J. Singer, W. Sturges, and E. Waddell. 2000. DeSoto Canyon eddy intrusion study. Final report, Volume II: Technical report. U.S. Dept. of the Interior, Minerals Management Service, Gulf of Mexico OCS Region, New Orleans, LA. OCS Study MMS 2000-080. 269 pp.

Hamilton P. and A. Lugo-Fernandez. 2001. Observation of high speed deep currents in the northern Gulf of Mexico. Geophys Res. Lett. July 2001.

Hamilton, P., T.J. Berger, and W. Johnson. In Press. On the structure and motions of cyclones in the northern Gulf of Mexico. J. Geophys. Res.,

He, D., D.R. Watts, and K.L. Tracey. 1998 Determining geostrophic velocity shear profiles with IESs. J. Geophys. Res. 103: 5607-5622.

Hogg, N.G. 1981. Topographic waves along 70°W on the continental rise. J. Mar. Res. 39: 627-649.

Hogg, N.G. 2000. Low-frequency variability on the western flanks of the Grand Banks. J. Mar. Res. 58: 523-545.

Howden, S.D., D.R. Watts, K.L. Tracey, and H.T. Rossby. 1994. An acoustic telemetry system implemented for real-time monitoring of the Gulf Stream with inverted echo sounders. J. Atmos Ocean. Tech. 11: 567-571.

Kelly, K.A. and D.R. Watts. 1994. An observational stream function in the Gulf Stream. J. Phys. Oceanogr. 24: 2321-2333.

Kirwan, A.D., W.J. Merrell, Jr., J.K. Lewis, and R.E. Whitaker. 1984. Lagrangian observations of an anticyclonic ring in the western Gulf of Mexico. J. Geophys.Res. 89(C3): 3417-3424.

Koopmans, L.H. 1974. The spectral analysis of time series. Academic 353 pp.

Kunze, E. 1985. Near-inertial wave propagationin geostrophic shear. J. Phys. Oceanogr. 15: 544-565.

Kunze, E. 1986. The mean and near-inertial velocity fields in a warm-core ring. J. Phys. Oceanogr. 16: 1444-1461.

LeBlond, P.H. and L.A. Mysack. 1978. Waves in the Ocean. Amsterdam: Elsevier.

Lighthill, M.J. 1978. Waves in fluids. Cambridge, MA: Cambridge University Press.

Malanotte-Rizzoli, P., D.B. Haidvogel, and R.E. Young. 1987. Numerical simulation of transient boundary-forced radiation. Part I: The linear regime. J. Phys. Oceanogr. 17: 1439-1457.

Meinen, C., E. Fields, R. Pickart, and D.R. Watts. 1993a. A test of the Parsons-Veronis hypothesis on the separation of the Gulf Stream. J. Phys. Oceanogr. 22: 1286-1301.

Meinen, C., E. Fields, R.S. Pickart, and D.R. Watts. 1993b. Ray tracing on topographic Rossby waves. Graduate School of Oceanography, Technical Report 93-1, University of Rhode Island. 43 pp.

Meinen C.S. and D.R. Watts. 2000. Calibrating inverted echo sounders equipped with pressure sensors. Journal of Atmospheric and Oceanic Technology. 15: 1339-1345.

Meinen, C.S. and D.R. Watts. 2000. Vertical structure and transport on a transect across the North Atlantic Current near 42N: Time series and mean. Journal of Geophysical Research 105: 21,869-21,891.

Mooers, C.N.K. 1975. Several effects of a baroclinic current on the cross-stream propagation of inertial-internal waves. Geophys. Fluid Dgn. 6: 245-275.

Munk, W.H. and D.E. Cartwright. 1965. Tidal spectroscopy and prediction. Philos. Trans. R. Soc. London. A, 259: 533-581.

Oey L.Y. and H.C. Lee. 2002. Deep eddy and topographic Rossby waves in the Gulf of Mexico. J. Phys. Oceanogr. 32: 3499-3527.

Pickart, R.S. 1995. Gulf Stream-generated topographic Rossby waves. J. Phys. Oceanogr. 25:574-584.

Priesendorfer, R.W. 1998. Principal component analysis in meteorology and oceanography. Development in Atmospheric Science. 17: Elsevier, NY. 425 pp.

Priestley, M.B. 1981. Spectral analysis and time series. London: Academic Press. 890 pp.

Rhines, P.B. 1970. Edge-, bottom-, and Rossby waves in a rotating stratified fluid. Geophys Fluid Dyn. 1: 273-302.

Shay, L.K. and R.L. Elsberry 1987. Near-inertial ocean current response to Hurricane "Frederic." J. Phys. Oceanogr. 17: 1249-1269.

Sun, C. and D.R. Watts. 2001. A gravest empirical mode analysis for the southern ocean hydrography. J. Geophys. Res. 106: 2833-2855.

Thompson, R.O.R.Y. 1977. Observations of Rossby waves near site D. Prog. Oceanogr. 7: 135-162.

Tracey, K.L. S.D. Howden, and D.R. Watts. 1997. IES calibration and mapping procedures. J. Atmos. Oceanic Technol. 14: 1483-1493.

Watts, D.R., C. Sun, and S. Rintoul. 2001. Gravest empirical modes determined from hydrographic observations in the subantarctic front. J.Phys. Oceanog. 31: 2186-2209.

The Department of the Interior Mission

As the Nation's principal conservation agency, the Department of the Interior has responsibility for most of our nationally owned public lands and natural resources. This includes fostering sound use of our land and water resources; protecting our fish, wildlife, and biological diversity; preserving the environmental and cultural values of our national parks and historical places; and providing for the enjoyment of life through outdoor recreation. The Department assesses our energy and mineral resources and works to ensure that their development is in the best interests of all our people by encouraging stewardship and citizen participation in their care. The Department also has a major responsibility for American Indian reservation communities and for people who live in island territories under U.S. administration.

The Minerals Management Service Mission

As a bureau of the Department of the Interior, the Minerals Management Service's (MMS) primary responsibilities are to manage the mineral resources located on the Nation's Outer Continental Shelf (OCS), collect revenue from the Federal OCS and onshore Federal and Indian lands, and distribute those revenues.

Moreover, in working to meet its responsibilities, the **Offshore Minerals Management Program** administers the OCS competitive leasing program and oversees the safe and environmentally sound exploration and production of our Nation's offshore natural gas, oil and other mineral resources. The MMS **Minerals Revenue Management** meets its responsibilities by ensuring the efficient, timely and accurate collection and disbursement of revenue from mineral leasing and production due to Indian tribes and allottees, States and the U.S. Treasury.

The MMS strives to fulfill its responsibilities through the general guiding principles of: (1) being responsive to the public's concerns and interests by maintaining a dialogue with all potentially affected parties and (2) carrying out its programs with an emphasis on working to enhance the quality of life for all Americans by lending MMS assistance and expertise to economic development and environmental protection.